POCKET GUIDE TO THE HUMANE CONTROL OF WILDLIFE IN CITIES & TOWNS

POCKET GUIDE TO THE HUMANE CONTROL OF WILDLIFE IN CITIES & TOWNS

Edited by Guy R. Hodge

Contributors: William Bridgeland,
Donald L. Burton, D.V.M.,
John W. Grandy, Ph.D.,
John Hadidian, Ph.D.,
Guy R. Hodge

Illustrated by Pat Herman
Technical drawings by
   Illustrations Unlimited

Guy R. Hodge is the director of the Department of Data and Information Services for The Humane Society of the United States.

William Bridgeland is an urban wildlife biologist who is self-employed as a pest-control operator in Baltimore, Maryland.

Donald L. Burton, M.S., D.V.M., is the founder and director of the Wildlife Rehabilitation and Research Cooperative in Columbus, Ohio.

John W. Grandy, Ph.D., is the vice president of Wildlife and Habitat Protection for The Humane Society of the United States.

John Hadidian, Ph.D., is an urban wildlife specialist with the National Park Service in Washington, D.C.

This book was originally brought to publication with the generous assistance of the Geraldine R. Dodge Foundation, which provided financial support to The HSUS urban wildlife programs through a grant that allowed us to print the pocket guide and to develop an exhibit for a series of seminars on "Humane Solutions to Problems with Urban Wildlife."

For additional copies, please write Falcon Press Publishing, P.O. Box 1718, Helena, MT 59624, or call toll-free, 1-800-582-2665. Don't forget to ask for a free catalog.

For information on membership in The Humane Society of the United States, see page 115.

TABLE OF CONTENTS

Each year, animal shelters receive calls for help from citizens who have encountered wild animals inside buildings or wandering about in yards. People seek help in coping with unwelcome wildlife tenants from nature centers, game wardens, and licensed wildlife rehabilitators. Many callers consider traditional pest-control products, such as poison bait and lethal traps, to be unpalatable. Citizens are no longer content just to rid their premises of troublesome wildlife; they want to accomplish this feat without harm to the animals.

Animal-control tactics that pose no threat to animals or the environment are fast becoming the tools of preference for this generation. The Humane Society of the United States, for the first time, has compiled in a single volume a collection of nonlethal approaches to wildlife-damage control. This pocket guide presents clear, straightforward instructions for the control of wild animals in cities and towns.

In most cases, the conflicts between wild animals and humans can be resolved without harm to living creatures. In fact, humane tactics for wildlife-damage control often are the cheapest and the most practical and lasting of solutions.

Many tactics for wildlife-damage control have been passed by word of mouth from generation to generation. The flower of the lavender plant, for example, is said to repel mice, and some people insist that glass bottles partially buried around a garden will frighten away rabbits. Many of these popular solutions to problems with wildlife have not been studied by biologists, and their usefulness is a matter of speculation. In selecting the tactics and tools discussed in this pocket guide, the authors attempted to limit their reviews to proven methods of wildlife-damage control. While some of our suggestions may seem unconventional, they are based on published research in combination with our knowledge of animal biology.

We do not have all the answers. Although Americans have come a long way in their attitudes toward animals and in their approach to wildlife management, there is still much to be learned about coexisting with wildlife in the urban environment. Readers are encouraged to share with The Humane Society of the United States their ideas and experiences in dealing with troublesome wild animals.

Guy R. Hodge

PREFACE

It is with a great sense of pride and pleasure, but mixed emotions, that I introduce this *Pocket Guide to the Humane Control of Wildlife in Cities and Towns*.

Unfortunately, the human world is closing in on the wildlife that we hold so dear. As our cities and towns grow and suburbs expand, there are inevitable conflicts between the perceived and legitimate needs of people and the needs of animals. For far too long, these conflicts have been "solved" merely by killing wildlife, sometimes extirpating whole populations of animals. Yet now, thankfully, a world that is awakening to the need for environmental quality and a livable planet is also demanding rational solutions to conflicts with wildlife.

Increasingly, at The Humane Society of the United States (HSUS), we get calls asking for "humane" solutions to wildlife problems. Most people no longer want to kill wildlife; they would rather live with it, not just because we are becoming a more humane and caring people, but because in a world of skyscrapers and one-acre lots there is an innate need to experience the joy of wild things: the antics of a squirrel, the drumming of a woodpecker, the call of a chickadee, the playfulness of a raccoon, or the gurgling cry of a crow. These vestiges of our wild heritage are things we need to treasure. Yet, inevitably, wherever wildlife and people get close together, there are problems.

This guide also marks a milestone for the animal-protection community. For years, The HSUS and other organizations have marched from one highly visible wildlife crisis to another. We have fought in the courts, in the Congress, and in the halls of government to save elephants, fur seals, endangered species, porpoises, whales, fur animals, wild birds, and predators and to save lands such as national wildlife refuges, national parks, wetlands, and other areas as habitats for wildlife. But while we were fighting these important battles, a quiet crisis was emerging, largely unnoticed. Community by community, and city by city, problems between people and wildlife were growing, but there was almost no assembled information on solutions that could provide the animals with the care and treatment that they deserve. Thus, this pocket guide is designed to address this quiet and growing crisis by providing citizens, humane societies, and animal-control personnel with a compendium of techniques for humanely solving wildlife/people problems, while enabling and encouraging people to live with all the joys and wonders that wild animals bring into our lives.

As the first pocket guide of its kind, there will be inevitable omissions and subsequent editions. Hopefully, the impact of the pocket guide and its successors will be pervasive and long-lasting in terms of encouraging animal protection nationwide.

As we enter the 1990s, with Earth Day and the attendant "regreening" of America's consciousness, it is our hope that this pocket guide will help—at least in a small way—to make this nation more livable and humane for both people and animals.

John W. Grandy
Vice President
Wildlife and Habitat Protection

THE TACTICS AND TOOLS OF ANIMAL-PROOFING

Nearly any wild animal, given the proper food source, water, and cover, can make a home among humans. When wild creatures get out of hand in the city or suburbs, it is usually because they have found a comfortable haven. People unwittingly provide food and shelter for wildlife; sometimes we are so accommodating that a colony of mammals or flock of birds will attain greater numbers than exist under natural conditions.

In most cases, the damage caused by wild animals is avoidable. There are few simple solutions to dealing with wild animals, but there are intelligent choices. The Humane Society of the United States preaches a concept called "animal-proofing." This common sense approach to animal-damage control can be achieved by physically excluding wildlife, conditioning them to avoid the area, or inhibiting their breeding. With a minimum of effort, humans can adapt to, or even choose, their animal neighbors.

There are a wide variety of tactics and tools that can be used to evict unwanted animals or to mitigate the damage they cause. The resources available to the public range from high-tech commercial devices to home remedies. There is no tactic that will work against all animals all of the time. Even when a tactic is fundamentally sound, it might fail because equipment was poorly constructed, incorrectly installed, or improperly maintained. And let us not forget the most important variable—the animal. A wild animal's response to any tactic can vary with the season of the year or the availability of alternative sources of food and shelter, as well as previous exposures to similar equipment. A realistic measure of success is whether these tactics, when used alone or in conjunction with each other, will reduce problems to acceptable levels.

In order to effectively deal with a trouble-causing wild animal, a person must understand the nature of the problem. The first step, for either the beleaguered citizen or the professional, is to carefully analyze the situation. The trick is to think like a wild animal. Our knowledge of animal behavior and natural history should be used to get at the heart of the problem and to select the proper approach for that situation.

Most wildlife is territorial; an individual animal remains in an area, its home range, because that site meets its requirements for food and shelter. In order to design a course of corrective action, a person must identify entryways, pathways, and food caches used by the animals. Once armed with this knowledge, a person can begin to explore a potential course of action.

The most important category of animal-damage-control tools is physical barriers that block an animal's access to a structure or parcel of land. Physical barriers are the only tools for animal-damage control that provide permanent relief and are preferred for most conflicts between people and wildlife.

Whenever wild animals invade human dwellings, the process of animal-proofing should start with repairs—replace or board up broken windows, mend torn screens, tightly fasten floor drains, and patch holes in outer walls. All holes and openings larger than ¼ inch should be blocked or screened with building materials resistant to gnawing or prying, such as galvanized sheet metal or heavy-gauge hardware cloth. Cracks in concrete and masonry should be patched with mortar.

Physical barriers take many forms, from commercial products to screens improvised from hardware supplies. The most popular commercial product is probably bird netting, a ready-made barrier constructed of weatherproof synthetic fiber that is used to exclude pigeons and other birds from structures, to prevent birds from roosting in trees, and to protect garden vegetables. Netting was originally developed to protect fruit crops, such as grapes and blueberries, from raids by birds. In tests, netting reduced bird damage to crops by 90–99 percent, and it is equally effective in ridding man-made structures of avian occupants.

Porcupine wire, as its name suggests, is a strip of metal with protruding prongs. It is also used in bird control, usually to pigeon-proof ledges, railings, and rooftops. Rather than excluding birds, porcupine wire transforms the contour of a surface so that the birds are no longer able to gain secure or comfortable footing. A handyman can obtain similar results by stringing monofilament line or galvanized wire along a ledge.

Sometimes, basic modifications in the design or shape of a structure will create an insurmountable obstacle to animals. Pigeons, for example, prefer to perch on a flat surface. When a ledge is sloped about 60 degrees, pigeons have difficulty maintaining their footing. An angled rail or beam can cause birds to slide off a ledge surface as they attempt to land.

The term repellents refers to materials that are offensive to an animal's sense of taste, smell, or touch. Repellents are useful in situations where the objective is to quickly and temporarily drive animals away from a site. Success in the use of these tools is measured in the reduction of damage, not in its total elimination. A repellent is best suited for such jobs as protecting vegetable gardens just long enough for the crop to be harvested.

More than 100 chemical repellents are currently marketed in the United States. There are twenty-five products registered just to repel deer. Moth balls, moth flakes, ammonium soaps, and bone tar oil are examples of compounds that produce odors offensive to animals. Human hair also qualifies as a repellent and is used to keep wild animals away from ornamental trees and vegetable gardens. A study conducted at a botanical garden in New York demonstrated that deer and rabbits associate the human scent with danger. When hair is placed in a nylon stocking or onion bag and hung on a tree, deer often will avoid that tree while browsing on nearby vegetation.

Some chemicals are formulated to change the taste of trees, shrubs, and flowers so that they are unpalatable to wild animals. In some cases, biologists are uncertain whether a chemical alters the taste of the plant, mildly irritates an animal's mouth, or upsets its stomach. Chemicals that affect an animal's sense of taste include coal tar, copper oxalate, thiram, and ziram. A popular homemade recipe for a taste repellent consists of 1 tablespoon of hot pepper sauce in a gallon of water, mixed with a commercial garden product that retards water evaporation in plants.

Any unnatural noise or movement can startle animals. Noisemaking devices are designed to convey messages of stress, alarm, or imminent danger to animals and should prompt animals to flee. Noisemaking equipment that can frighten wildlife includes wind chimes, portable radios, recordings of animal distress calls and predator calls, and custom-made firecrackers. Objects that create a visual repellent or a frightening movement include mirrors, pie tins, flood and strobe lights, flares, lanterns, revolving lights, flags, balloons, scarecrows, kites, and strips of foil.

One of the keys to success with scare devices is to take action at the first sign of a problem. It is difficult to break an animal's patterns of behavior or movement once they have been established. One problem with scare tactics is that animals can become accustomed to a sight or sound, and, after a period of time, they will ignore it or retreat only a short distance. The best results are obtained by simultaneously employing different types of tactics, as well as moving or changing scare tools and methods to prevent the wildlife from becoming conditioned to them.

It is also possible to condition wild animals to avoid a site by punishing them for incursions. An electrified fence delivers a mild, but irritating, electrical shock to an animal that comes into contact with a wire. Two conductors embedded in a cable carry a pulsating electric charge away from the power unit, commonly a 110-volt battery. An animal that touches the cable completes an electrical circuit and receives a high-voltage, low-amperage shock that should not cause injury. Electrified fencing can be used to keep wild animals out of a garden, yard, or pasture.

The urban landscape can be altered to reduce the food, water, and cover available to animals. Secretive animals, such as mice and snakes, can sometimes be driven from the land by taking steps to eliminate protective cover. The process can be as simple as elevating a stack of firewood off the ground or stuffing a pile of brush into a trash can. Trimming a tree branch that overhangs the roof of a house will keep a squirrel or raccoon from using the tree as a ladder to an attic den.

One of the most common methods of wildlife-damage control involves the use of cage traps to capture animals unharmed and relocate them into wooded areas. Often, these wild places do not provide a haven for displaced wild animals. Most habitat areas already are providing home for as many creatures as can be supported by the available food and shelter. There may be no room for another raccoon, squirrel, or other animal. At best, an animal that is uprooted and moved into unfamiliar territory is at a disadvantage in competing with other wildlife for food or living space.

Many relocated animals become nomads. Raccoons have been tracked traveling well over 100 miles from their release sites. Uprooted animals do not live very long; about 50 percent of relocated raccoons die within three months of their release. Many of these creatures are crushed under the wheels of automobiles as they cross highways in seach of a place to live.

Sometimes homeowners are faced with hard choices about accommodating wildlife within the boundaries of their properties. The animal's best hope for survival is where it already lives. In most instances, once steps are taken to keep the wild animal out of the house, garbage, and garden, it can peaceably coexist with the homeowner. Unless the property is animal-proofed, live trapping is fruitless, since the unoccupied territory will provide an open invitation for another animal to take up residence.

Urban wildlife owe their existence, in part, to the generosity of man. Not only do some animals accept handouts, they pilfer food from bird feeders and refuse containers, and they use inedible items as nesting material. Animals tend to concentrate in areas where people feed them. Problems with wildlife often can be solved just by taking steps to assure the proper storage, collection, and disposal of refuse.

Wildlife-damage control is as much an art as it is a science. The successful management of any wild animal depends upon a mixture of skill, timing, ingenuity, diligence, and a degree of tolerance. By applying the techniques discussed in this pocket guide, people should be able to head off most problems with wildlife.

Of course, there is really nothing novel about animal-proofing. For years, many professionals have preached that good sanitation and building maintenance will resolve most problems with wild animals. The concept has not had much of a chance to take hold. What is new is that wildlife managers, humane society officials, animal-control officers, and wildlife rehabilitators have now begun working together to promote a responsible approach to wildlife-damage control.

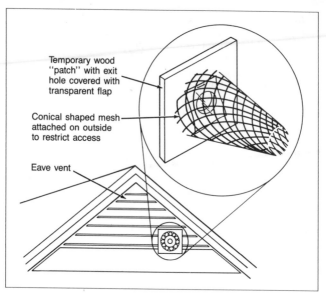

Temporary wood "patch" with exit hole covered with transparent flap

Conical shaped mesh attached on outside to restrict access

Eave vent

FIGURE 1: BAT EXCLUDER

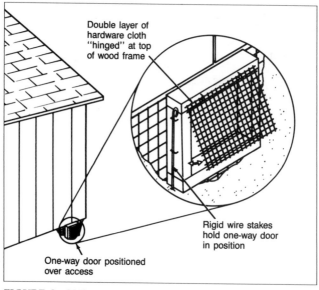

Double layer of hardware cloth "hinged" at top of wood frame

Rigid wire stakes hold one-way door in position

One-way door positioned over access

FIGURE 2: ONE-WAY DOOR

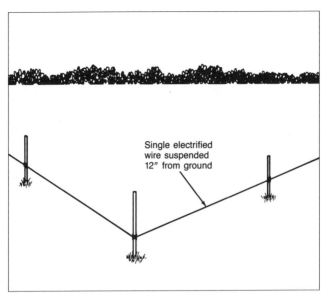

FIGURE 3: ELECTRIC FENCE

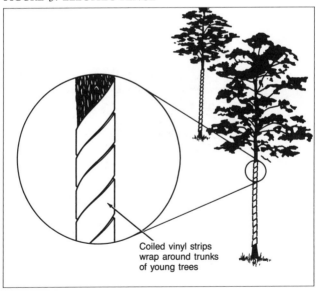

FIGURE 4: TREE GUARD

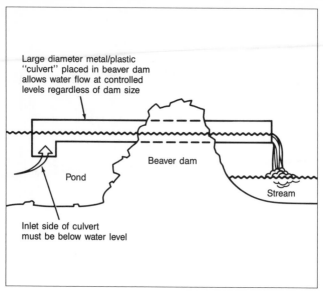

Large diameter metal/plastic "culvert" placed in beaver dam allows water flow at controlled levels regardless of dam size

Beaver dam

Pond

Stream

Inlet side of culvert must be below water level

FIGURE 5: BEAVER CULVERT

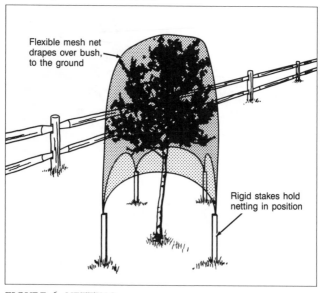

Flexible mesh net drapes over bush, to the ground

Rigid stakes hold netting in position

FIGURE 6: NETTING

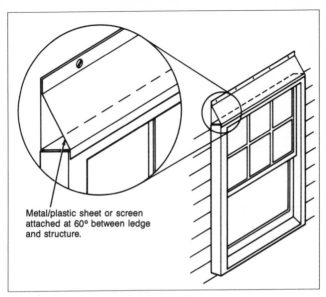

FIGURE 7: SLOPED LEDGE GUARD

Metal/plastic sheet or screen attached at 60° between ledge and structure.

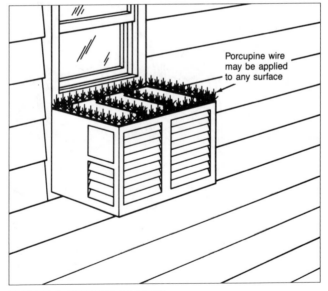

FIGURE 8: PORCUPINE WIRE

Porcupine wire may be applied to any surface

THE TACTICS AND TOOLS OF ANIMAL-PROOFING 11

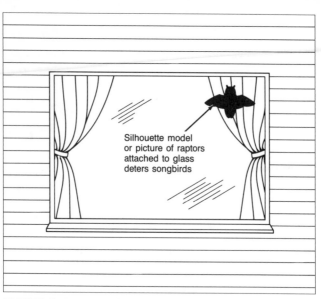

FIGURE 9: SILHOUETTE OF A RAPTOR

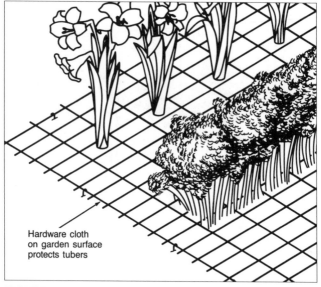

FIGURE 10: HARDWARE GROUND CLOTH

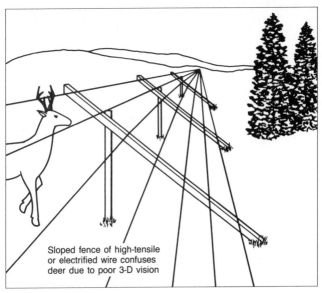

Sloped fence of high-tensile or electrified wire confuses deer due to poor 3-D vision

FIGURE 11: HIGH TENSILE FENCE

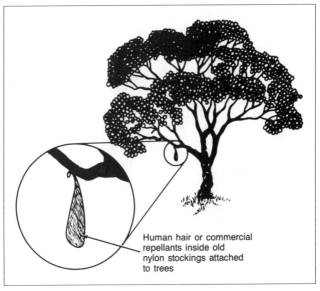

Human hair or commercial repellants inside old nylon stockings attached to trees

FIGURE 12: HUMAN HAIR

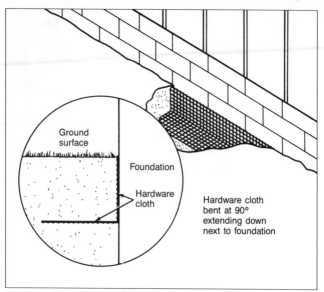

FIGURE 13: FOUNDATION SKIRT

Ground surface

Foundation

Hardware cloth

Hardware cloth bent at 90° extending down next to foundation

FIGURE 14: BALLOON

A plastic "eyespot" balloon, hanging from a swivel pole

The armadillo is recognized principally by its protective body armor, with distinctive rings between shoulders and hips. The long tail is also armored, and the head is narrow and ends in a blunt snout. On average, armadillos are slightly larger than house cats.

ARMADILLOS

NATURAL HISTORY

Habitat—Armadillos are found throughout the south, from Texas to Florida, but do not range farther north than Kansas. Although armadillos prefer heavy brush or woodlands, they can live in areas of less cover, provided there is moisture and loose, sandy loam soils in which they prefer to burrow.

Diet—By far, the bulk of the armadillo's diet is composed of insects and larvae. Plant foods are eaten occasionally, as are small reptiles.

Breeding—Breeding usually occurs in the late fall, with a long gestation period resulting in births in March and April. Armadillos are unique in that the young are usually born as identical quadruplets, derived from a single egg (ovum) and genetically alike.

LEGAL STATUS

Armadillos are not protected in most states, but local ordinances should always be consulted before action is taken against animals.

PUBLIC HEALTH

Although armadillos can be infected with the bacterium that causes human leprosy, there is no indication that they are involved in the transmission of any disease to humans.

TYPES OF DAMAGE

Armadillos cause occasional damage to crops and can be a nuisance in vegetable and flower gardens by uprooting plants in their search for insects and earthworms. They may also burrow under buildings or other structures.

Exclusion—Armadillos can be kept out of places where they are not wanted by fencing, although special designs may be necessary given their ability to climb. Local extension specialists should be consulted if fencing is to be considered.

Habitat Modification—Brush should be removed where it is thick enough to provide cover or where burrows are known to exist. Control of insects or other invertebrates may remove the major food sources and help in keeping armadillos from becoming established in an area.

Trapping—Armadillos can be live-trapped using spoiled meat or overripe fruit as a bait. Trapping is most successful around burrows. Animals should be moved to suitable habitat at least two miles distant. As always, trapping should be viewed as a last resort and care should be taken to avoid using this technique when young are being raised (March through September).

BATS

There are almost forty species of bats in the United States, each with its distinctive physical characteristics. The few species likely to be encountered by people live in colonies, and the following general statements apply to them. Bats are the only mammals capable of active flight and are often mistaken as birds when seen flying. They can be distinguished by their butterfly-like wing beat, lack of long tail and beak, and typically nighttime activity. A close view reveals their furry brown bodies, large ears, and mostly bare wing membranes. The wingspan of the common species is from 6–10 inches.

Habitat—Bats that people are likely to encounter are those that roost in or on buildings, either singly or in colonies, in urban and suburban areas, wherever there are substantial populations of flying insects. Bats are most numerous around ponds, lakes, and rivers. They are most active in the warmer months, and in much of the country they migrate or hibernate to avoid winter cold.

Diet—All common North American bats feed on insects, which they catch in flight with their mouths, wings, or tail membranes. They detect their prey by echolocation, which is the remarkable ability to emit high frequency sounds (outside of human hearing) and discern objects by the sound they reflect back to the bat. Different bat species specialize in eating different types of insects. Bats are considered beneficial since a single bat may eat over half its own weight in insects each night.

Breeding—Depending on the latitude, bats give birth to their single baby (occasionally twins) in early to late May, with the young unable to fly until early to late July. The newborn of some species clings to its mother while she hunts, but all offspring are left behind in the nursery colony as they grow too large to be carried. Attics are often used as nurseries because the warmth benefits the growing babies.

LEGAL STATUS

In most states, bats are classified as protected nongame species. A bat may not be harmed except under the special conditions set by the game department. The regulations governing the control of bats can be obtained from the local game warden.

PUBLIC HEALTH

A small percentage of bats may carry rabies, which could be transmitted to humans or pets by a bite if a bat is handled improperly. Accumulated bat droppings may harbor histoplasmosis fungi spores, which can cause respiratory illness if stirred up and inhaled. Small amounts of droppings in attics are best left undisturbed, but if cleanup is necessary, an adequate dust mask should be worn.

TYPES OF DAMAGE

Since bats are unable to gnaw or dig, they must rely on existing openings to enter buildings. Property damage is usually very minor and associated with stains and odors from accumulated urine and feces. The presence of these gentle and beneficial creatures flying in someone's yard is no cause for alarm in itself. Remedial action is only appropriate if a bat is discovered inside a building. Two general situations are typical: a bat in the living space of a building, and a bat or bats residing in an attic, wall, or other area of a building outside of the living space.

Bat in living space—Residents discover a bat flying through the house (usually in the evening) or roosting on a curtain, furniture, etc.

Bats in residence—These are often first noticed as they are seen leaving the building at dusk, or their rustlings or vocalizations are heard in the walls or ceiling. (Similar nocturnal noises may also be caused by mice or flying squirrels.) A bat in the living space may indicate that a colony is in the attic. Occasionally the first sign of bats is a brown, odorous stain appearing on the ceiling or wall. Droppings may also accumulate under the bat entrance on the exterior of the building. Droppings are dry cylinders about ¼ inch long, made of iridescent pieces of insect shells.

CONTROL METHODS

Bat in living space—Do not panic! The bat will not attack or hurt anyone! The bat does not want to be in the house and is trying to find a way out. The best thing to do is to close interior doors, confine it to a room if possible, and give it an exit by opening a door or window. If the bat is still flying, it will probably circle the room a few times, locate the exit with its sonar, and depart. If the bat disappears before an exit has been provided, it probably has landed somewhere it can hang easily, e.g., behind curtains or upholstered furniture, on hanging clothes, or in house plants. If it cannot be found, leave the exit open and accessible, turn out the lights, and wait. If it is nighttime, the bat should leave shortly. Otherwise, it should leave within an hour of nightfall.

A bat that has landed may be captured and released outside. If it is hanging on a curtain or other vertical surface, carefully place a jar or can over it, gently work it into the container, and cover it quickly. A bat on the floor can be covered with a thick towel and gathered up for transport. Leather (not cotton) work gloves are adequate protection from a bat's small teeth and will allow a person to safely pick up a bat. Never try to handle a bat with bare hands. Be prepared for the bat to squeal loudly in protest when picked up.

After the bat has been freed, it is important to find out how the bat entered the house. It is possible that it came in an open door or window, but that is seldom the case. It is more likely that it had been roosting somewhere within the outer walls of the house and accidently found a route to the living space. Common entry points include gaps around window air conditioners, chimneys, and openings in interior walls that lead to attics or cellars that may harbor more bats. Seal these entrances immediately unless there is some reason to suspect that there may be other bats still inside, in which case proceed to the next section of this guide.

Bats in residence—The most likely place for a bat colony to become established in a house is the attic. The key to excluding a bat colony from a building is to find any and all openings that the bats are using. A well-used opening will usually be smudged on the outside and have droppings below it, but not always. Some bats can enter cracks as small as $3/8$ inch, so inspect the house closely. Careful observation of suspected entrances at dusk can confirm use by the bats as they leave to hunt for the night. Watch closely from before sunset until at least thirty minutes after sunset; it only takes a fraction of a second for a bat to exit and take flight.

The basic strategy for removing a bat colony from a building is to allow the bats to leave on their own but to deny them reentry. The use of poisons or repellents is not recommended because they are either ineffective, dangerous to people, or may serve to drive bats deeper into the house where they may enter the living space or die in the walls and create an odor problem. Even if poisons did work on the existing bats, others would eventually move in if the basic problem of the opening was not solved.

Bats should only be evicted from a building when no immature animals are likely to be present (early spring, late summer, and fall). From late May to August there may be bats too young to fly and that would be trapped inside where they would eventually die and possibly cause an odor problem. Bat colonies discovered during this period should be tolerated until August. In the meantime, potential bat access to the interior living space of the house should be sealed up from the inside.

Once all entrances have been located, seal all except the largest or most obvious entrance(s) with appropriate building materials. This last entrance should then be fitted with a bat excluder or one-way door (see figs. 1 and 2). Leave the door in place for several nights to give all bats a chance to exit. If possible, check the attic to be sure there are no bats left, and watch the outside of the house in the evening again to make sure the bats have not found another way in. If they have, move the one-way door to the new entrance. After the bats are gone, remove the door and seal the last opening.

BEAVERS

The beaver, with an average weight of about 40 pounds, is the largest North American rodent. The animal is recognized principally by its flat, paddle-like tail and webbed feet. Beaver fur varies in color from reddish blonde to dark brown.

NATURAL HISTORY

Habitat—Beavers commonly reside in rivers, lakes, streams, and other aquatic environments that contain an adequate flow of water for damming. Beavers may reside either in lodges built from branches, mud, and other debris or in dens dug into the banks of streams or lakes.

Diet—Like other rodents, the beaver's incisor teeth grow constantly. The animal must continually gnaw against trees or its incisors will penetrate its skull. Beavers build piles of food, called "caches," from the branches of deciduous trees. The caches are located underwater for use as winter food when the pond is frozen. When feeding on branches, beavers eat only the bark and cambium layer. During the summer months, beavers feed primarily on aquatic vegetation.

Breeding—The female produces one litter per year, usually between March and June. A typical litter contains three or four kits. The young become sexually mature by the age of one and a half years. A beaver colony commonly contains eight to thirteen animals including an adult pair, the kits from the previous spring, and the yearlings. In spring, the yearlings leave the lodge to form their own colonies. The dispersing beavers travel an average distance of 7 miles in search of new homes.

LEGAL STATUS

In most states beavers are classified as a game species.

PUBLIC HEALTH

Giardiasis can be spread through the fecal matter of aquatic mammals including the beaver.

TYPES OF DAMAGE

The greatest concern of homeowners and farmers is that the land behind a beaver dam can become flooded. Burrowing activity can cause damage to shorelines. When beavers move into suburban areas, they sometimes will destroy ornamental trees and shrubs. The animals are particularly fond of willow and aspen trees. Beavers will sometimes gnaw the bark from evergreens to get at the sap, thereby exposing the underlayer of the trunk. The tree may be unable to survive the damage, which can be a 2 foot wide wound encircling the tree.

CONTROL METHODS

Exclusion—Beavers can be excluded from a parcel of land by means of a metal fence. Where a conventional fence is not practical or desirable, it may be possible to repel beavers with an electrified suspension fence that generates a high-voltage, low-amperage charge (see fig. 3). A single wire is suspended approximately one foot off the ground. When a beaver touches the wire, it receives a mild shock but is otherwise unharmed. After several encounters with the fence, the beaver will avoid that location.

Ornamental trees can be shielded from beavers by wrapping each one in hardware cloth, wire mesh, or tree wrap extending about 3½ feet above the ground (see fig. 4). The mesh size should be ¼–1 inch. If the trees are in an area that is occasionally flooded, the height of the cloth should be extended at least 2 feet above the high water mark.

Culverts—Destruction of a dam is futile. Beaver will begin rebuilding as soon as the landowner departs. It is possible, however, to modify a beaver dam so that the animals are unable to stem the flow of water. A pipe system, called a culvert, is placed through the dam (see fig. 5). This structural device regulates the water level and prevents beavers from expanding the size of a pond or impeding the flow of a stream.

The culvert must be of sufficient length to stick out well beyond the actual dam construction, particularly on the upstream side of the pond. A 10–40 foot culvert will be required for most dams. The pipe must be a minimum of 8–12 inches in diameter.

Either galvanized pipe, plastic pipe, or aluminum irrigation pipe can be used to construct the culvert. A culvert can also be built with concrete reinforcing-mesh panels and welded-wire mesh, or fashioned from boards of metal, wood, or fiber with the bottom side made of wire mesh. The culvert should be placed at the same depth as the water level that the landowner wants to maintain. Approximately five steel posts will be needed to position the culvert at the proper height.

Beavers will dam the mouth of a conventional culvert, so the side facing the beaver pond should be fitted with a protective cover called a "beaver baffler." A triangular wire guard should prevent beavers from placing materials flush against the mouth of the culvert.

Another type of baffler, shaped like an elbow bent downward at a 90 degree angle, can be fitted over the mouth of the culvert. The baffler protrudes approximately 1 foot under the water surface. Beavers will not be able to block the vertical intake opening of the culvert. Holes 1 inch in size, about 1 foot apart, can be drilled along the first 10 feet of culvert to further confuse the beavers.

In some cases beavers succeed in blocking existing culverts that were improperly installed or are in disrepair. This problem can be corrected by inserting a second pipe system inside the original culvert. The new pipe should be approximately 4 inches smaller in diameter than the original.

Habitat Modification—On many streams and ponds, beavers can be encouraged to relocate simply by removing food trees—particularly young willow and cottonwood trees—and dam construction material from the water's edge. Beavers are limited in their ability to haul building materials across land. In the absence of a ready supply of food or construction materials, beavers will be unable to colonize a stream or pond.

Repellents—A homemade concoction consisting of 1 tablespoon of hot pepper sauce in a gallon of water can be sprayed or painted on tree trunks to reduce gnawing damage by beavers. The compound must periodically be reapplied throughout the warm months when beavers are active.

Trapping—The beaver's size, strength, and sharp incisors enable it to escape from a standard cage trap. A special beaver trap has been designed in the shape of a giant purse with chain sides. Not only is a beaver trap expensive, about $150, but it takes skill to properly set it. If the trap is placed too deep in the water the animal may drown, and if it is not positioned correctly, the trap jaws may strike a beaver, causing fatal injuries. It is unlikely, moreover, that a trapper will be able to catch all the members of a colony and move the family together. It can be especially difficult to catch the kits since they may be hidden deep inside a burrow that can be 20 feet long and up to 4 feet beneath the surface.

Sparrows, starlings, and pigeons are the most troublesome of the birds commonly found in the urban environment. The common pigeon of city parks is about 11 inches long, with a white rump and dark tail band. The starling can be recognized by its speckled, iridescent plummage. The house sparrow, which is actually classifed as a weaver finch, is a small, brown-colored bird. The male is recognized by his black bib.

Habitat—Pigeons and sparrows each gather in flocks, but neither rivals the starlings, which in winter gather in large, noisy roosts sometimes numbering more than a million birds. Pigeons favor the downtown areas of cities while starlings and sparrows are equally at home in city parks and suburban

ROOSTING BIRDS

NATURAL HISTORY

yards. Each of these birds is an opportunist. They will nest in abandoned buildings, vents, under bridges, and in just about any other protected space into which a nest will fit.

Diet—In the urban environment, the birds subsist on a combination of handouts, seed from feeders, and garbage.

Breeding—Pigeons breed throughout the year, even during winter. The female lays a clutch of two eggs eight to twelve days after mating. About eighteen days later the eggs hatch.

LEGAL STATUS

The house sparrow, pigeon, and starling are introduced species. These are classified as "unprotected" species, and there are few restrictions on their control.

PUBLIC HEALTH

The infectious diseases attributed to pigeons include histoplasmosis, toxoplasmosis, psittacosis, cryptococcosis, salmonellosis, meningitis, tuberculosis, and encephalitis. In fact, there is little evidence linking pigeons to infections in humans. Birds do, however, play a substantial role in the transmission of one infectious disease—histoplasmosis.

TYPES OF DAMAGE

The main complaint against starlings, sparrows, and pigeons is that, in areas where they congregate, their droppings create a foul-smelling, unsightly mess.

CONTROL METHODS

Exclusion—Netting is the tool of choice for many conflicts with roosting birds (see fig. 6). Netting can be used to exclude birds from virtually any type of structure, from a detached house to an office building. Nets can also be used to prevent birds from roosting or nesting in trees and to protect garden vegetables. The net will not entangle birds. It is made of a material that will not corrode, rot, or rust, and it is resistant to most cleaning solvents used in building maintenance.

To evict birds from window ledges, the netting is anchored to the roof, draped across the front of the structure, and then tightly secured to the base and sides of the building. Netting can be used under bridges or inside buildings where pigeons perch on beams, girders, struts, and supports. The netting can be suspended below the perches to create a false ceiling that excludes the birds. Netting can also be used to secure loading dock doors and other entryways that must remain open. The netting is installed in overlapping strips so as to form a protective curtain that parts to allow the passage of personnel and vehicles and then falls back into place to seal out pigeons.

Openings to lofts, vents, and eaves can be blocked with wire screens, netting, metal, or glass.

Pigeons prefer to perch on a flat surface. Wood, stone, or metal sheathing can be cut to the proper angle and fastened to a ledge so as to tilt the surface (see fig. 7). If the angle of the ledge is adjusted to 60 degrees or greater, it no longer provides secure footing, and birds will slide off the surface when they land.

Monofilament line or stainless-steel wire can be rigged to exclude pigeons from ledges, railings, awnings, and rooftops. A fence-like barrier can be created by stringing the wire several inches above the surface and anchoring it with eyelet screws. To keep the wire taut so it will not yield under a bird's weight, support posts should be placed at intervals of 6–18 inches along the length of the barrier. Electricity can be used to enhance the effectiveness of a wire barrier, but in most circumstances it is an unnecessary refinement.

Habitat Modification—Porcupine wire is particularly suitable for use on ledges or railings where birds roost (see fig. 8). It is laid in parallel rows and fastened to a surface with nails, screws, or adhesive. Birds are unable to maintain their footing on the metal strips and, therefore, avoid sites where this product is installed. Despite its menacing appearance, porcupine wire apparently is harmless to birds. The distress caused by the wire has been likened to trying to sleep on a bed of nails.

Habitat manipulation can be used where starlings congregate in roosts. Thinning branches will remove perch sites and reduce wind protection, forcing the birds to move to another site.

Food provided by picnickers, pedestrians, and devoted bird feeders is one of the factors affecting the abundance of pigeons and, to a lesser extent, starlings and sparrows. In some urban parks, handouts account for as much as three-quarters of the birds' diets. Birds frequent the parking lots of fast-food restaurants, city parks, trash dumps, and livestock feedlots. Curbing such handouts can be the single most important step in bird-proofing a home.

Trapping—In most situations it is impractical for a homeowner or building manager to trap birds.

Birth Control—A single chemosterilant, Ornitrol, is registered for the control of pigeons. Ornitrol produces temporary sterility in pigeons and inhibits the embryos from forming within eggs.

Studies indicate that Ornitrol can cause debilitating illness or death in some pigeons. The use of this drug, therefore, should be restricted to situations where a municipality insists on a chemical because of ease of application and where poisons are the only form of control that city officials will consider.

Ornitrol will not provide immediate relief from chronic problems, since the remaining birds will continue to congregate at spots offering perches or handouts of food. Moreover, it must be administered at all locations in the city where pigeons gather in large numbers.

Repellents—Scare tactics offer yet another approach to the control of pigeons. Noisemaking devices, for example, are disturbing to birds. A sudden, loud report, such as one produced by a shotgun or firecracker, can startle birds and frighten them into abandoning a roost or nest. A variety of commercial pyrotechnic devices are designed for use in bird control. Portable AM/FM stereo radios and wind chimes have also been used successfully to frighten birds. Noisemaking devices, to be effective, must be used persistently until the birds have established themselves elsewhere.

Visual stimuli such as mirrors, pie tins, revolving lights, colored flags, reflecting tape, and balloons can also be used to frighten birds. Visual and audible stimuli work best when combined to simultaneously assault both the birds' senses of sight and hearing.

Lifelike replicas of hawks, snakes, and owls are widely used to discourage pigeons from roosting or feeding. The effectiveness of these devices varies with the target species, the type of predator used as the model, and even the placement of the device. Regardless of the combination used, however, over time the target birds become accustomed to the replica and cease to fear it. In some cases this habituation can occur in as short a period as five to eight hours!

SONGBIRDS

This section contains a discussion of unique problems involving common songbirds. These are usually very minor problems in the sense that they result in no significant property damage or health threat, but they can be very puzzling, as well as annoying, to people experiencing them. Understanding the basis for the bird behavior that leads to these problems is essential in order to deal with them effectively.

LEGAL STATUS

Most songbirds (except house sparrows, starlings, and pigeons) are protected by state and federal laws.

PUBLIC HEALTH

Songbirds are not considered to be a significant source for any infectious disease that can be transmitted to humans.

TYPES OF DAMAGE

Songbird problems discussed in this section include: birds hitting windows; birds attacking people or pets; birds (chimney swifts) nesting in chimneys; birds singing at night.

Birds Hitting Windows—There are two types of situations that lead to birds hitting windows. The first results from the bird simply not seeing the glass and attempting to fly through it. This is most likely to happen with large picture windows, when the bird can see through part of the building to the yard beyond, or when large potted houseplants are visible through the window. A fast-flying bird may injure or kill itself when it strikes the glass, but if it survives one crash, it will usually not make the mistake again. To prevent this problem, the window needs to be made more visible to the birds. This may be done by closing shades or drapes, placing strips of masking tape on the glass, or applying decals of hawk or owl silhouettes to the glass (see fig. 9). These are available at nature centers and nature book stores.

The second situation leading to birds hitting windows is indicated by an individual bird, often a cardinal or robin, repeatedly pecking and/or flying into one or several windows. The bird sees its reflection in the glass, thinks it is an intruder on its territory, and attacks it to try to drive it away. It almost always occurs during the nesting season. The bird is *not* trying to get into the house. Usually, the bird does not injure itself seriously, but its repeated attacks may be very disturbing to the people in the house. The glass will reflect when it is darker inside the house than outside, so one strategy may be to place a bright light just inside the window. Drawing light-colored shades or drapes may also reduce the reflection, but temporarily covering the outside of the glass with a screen, cloth, or paper for perhaps a week is usually more effective.

Birds Attacking People or Pets— Certain birds that commonly nest close to human activity are extremely protective of the area around their nest, particularly after the nestlings have hatched. The adults will scold and fly at anything they consider a potential threat. Mockingbirds and barn swallows account for many of these attacks, but certain individuals of other species may also defend their nests this way. While an agitated bird diving at a person may be very intimidating, these attacks seldom result in the bird actually hitting or harming anyone. The bird is only interested in driving away the intruder and will not risk injury to itself. The best remedy for this situation is to simply avoid the area that the bird is defending for the three weeks or so that it takes for the baby birds to fledge, after which the parent usually stops being so aggressive. Pets will learn to do the same or may just ignore the bird's attacks. If avoidance is not practical, passing through the defended area while waving a cloth, or carrying an open umbrella or a broom overhead will at least keep the bird at a more comfortable distance.

Birds Nesting in Chimneys—There is a species of bird called the chimney swift that has adapted to nesting and roosting in chimneys. These birds have the remarkable ability to build nests made of sticks and saliva on the vertical surface of the inside of masonry chimneys, and they choose to roost inside chimneys, sometimes in large numbers, during their annual migration flights. They usually spend all of the daylight hours flying, catching insects to eat, and may be seen entering a chimney at dusk. The chimney swift is a beneficial species that is harmless to humans and causes few, if any, problems for homeowners. If swifts must be excluded from a chimney, it should be done outside the breeding season, which is May through August. When no nestlings are present, the birds may be easily excluded by screening the chimney during the day while they are out feeding.

Birds Singing at Night—There is one species of suburban songbird that is common in the south central and southeastern United States and is expanding its range northward to the lower Great Lakes and New England, that commonly sings loudly at night during the spring and summer. This is the mockingbird, well known for its ability to mimic the songs of other birds and a variety of other sounds that it hears. Its singing is a pleasure most of the time, but it may be quite annoying outside a bedroom window in the middle of the night. This may be a difficult problem to solve. Fortunately that nighttime singing is usually only done during a brief time of the year. Singing is often done from a favorite perch, and it may be possible to train the bird to avoid the perch by repeatedly scaring it away. A hose can be used to direct a *gentle* spray of water at the bird. One of the reasons mockingbirds sing is to defend food sources such as berry bushes and trees from other birds, and if such a food source is close to where the bird is singing, it may be helpful (although tedious) to pick and remove all the berries, leaving nothing for it to defend. If neither of these things work, and the singing is intolerable, earplugs may be the best option.

EASTERN CHIPMUNKS

This handsome and active rodent is actually a small (8–10 inches long) ground squirrel. The predominant background color of its fur is reddish brown, with several black and white stripes running down its back. Its furry tail is often carried straight up while it dashes for cover.

NATURAL HISTORY

Habitat—Chipmunks favor deciduous forests and brushy wood edges. They readily adapt to suburban gardens with natural landscaping and prefer to burrow in and around rock piles, wood piles, retaining walls, and fallen logs. They can easily climb trees, but they spend most of their time foraging along the ground. Chipmunks are active by day.

Diet—Chipmunks are largely plant eaters; acorns, nuts, other seeds, and berries make up the bulk of their diet. They also eat occasional insects, small amphibians, and, in rare instances, birds. Their foraging is most intense in the fall as they are gathering food stuffed in their cheek pouches to store in caches for the winter. They sleep through most of the winter but awake periodically to eat stored food.

Breeding—Mating begins as chipmunks emerge from their winter sleep in early spring (late February to early April) and again in early summer, to produce two litters of four to five young a year. The young emerge from their burrows after about six weeks and set out on their own within another two weeks.

LEGAL STATUS

In some states chipmunks are classified as a protected nongame species. A chipmunk may not be harmed except under the special conditions set by the game department. The regulations governing the control of chipmunks can be obtained from the local game warden.

PUBLIC HEALTH

Chipmunks are not considered to be a significant source for any infectious disease that can be transmitted to humans.

TYPES OF DAMAGE

Chipmunks do not usually cause property damage, with the occasional exception of injury to certain ornamental bulb plants that they may eat. Other animals, particularly mice and voles, also damage bulbs, while the more conspicuous chipmunks may get blamed. Some people get annoyed by their habit of burrowing in flower beds or under sidewalks and porches. Their burrows are usually not extensive enough to cause structural damage, and they rarely enter buildings for any reason. Chipmunk burrows are approximately 2 inches in diameter, have very little or no loose dirt around them, and usually plunge steeply downward.

Most people consider the enjoyment they get from watching these attractive animals as outweighing any nuisance they may cause. Considering the difficulty of keeping chipmunks out of suitable habitat, tolerance is probably the most prudent attitude.

Exclusion—Chipmunks may be kept from burrowing around sidewalks, porches, and retaining walls by burying hardware cloth "skirts" that extend down underground about 10 inches and flare out another 8 inches. Flower bulbs may be protected from burrowing chipmunks if planted beneath a wire screen ground cover, which allows plants to sprout through the mesh but prevents digging (see fig. 10).

Habitat Modification—Chipmunks may be discouraged from a yard by removing attractants such as wood and rock piles, dense ground covers, and brushy hedgerows.

Trapping—Live trapping chipmunks is not recommended for several reasons: removal of one chipmunk merely provides a vacant territory for another to occupy; it would take a tremendous effort to actually reduce the neighborhood population; release of a small animal like a chipmunk into unfamiliar territory with no burrow spells almost certain death due to predators, starvation, or accidents; and female chipmunks are raising dependent young during most of their active season, and removal of a mother chipmunk means death to her babies.

COYOTES

In form and body dimensions, coyotes resemble medium-sized dogs. Although coat color varies from almost white to a blackish gray, it is usually a medium gray with lighter color on the belly. Females are typically smaller than males, with adults averaging 35–40 pounds.

NATURAL HISTORY

Habitat—Coyotes are found throughout most of the continental United States, Central America, Canada, and Alaska. Their range is still expanding into parts of the eastern states. Coyotes live in many different habitats, including forest, grasslands, deserts, brushland, and mountains. Tolerant and able to adjust to people, coyotes are increasing their presence in suburban and even urban areas.

Diet—Coyotes eat a variety of plant and animal foods, including many raised by humans. They can be significant predators of livestock and will occasionally kill small domestic pets. To their credit, however, coyotes rely on rodents and rabbits for the major portion of their diet.

Breeding—Coyotes usually breed in February and March and give birth in April and May. The average litter contains six pups. The young are born in a den and first emerge at about three weeks of age. Weaning occurs by about two months of age.

LEGAL STATUS

The coyote may be classified either as an unprotected species or game animal. Most state wildlife codes allow coyotes to be killed when caught in the act of attacking livestock. In states where the coyote is listed as a game species, the animals may be hunted and trapped only under the conditions set by the game department.

Coyotes, like all warm-blooded animals, may contract rabies, but the coyote is not among the primary carriers of the disease.

The damage caused by coyotes is difficult to distinguish from free-roaming and feral dogs. Coyotes will raid garbage cans in urban areas as well as prey on livestock in rural areas.

Livestock/Poultry—Where small flocks of livestock or poultry need protection, penning or confinement can be effective. Electric or other specialized fencing can also be used on the advice of local extension specialists. Various modifications in husbandry practices, such as confining livestock during the birthing season, avoiding the use of pastures where predation has been high, and using guard dogs or herders to protect flocks, have also proven useful and may be considered after careful study and evaluation of a problem.

Crops—Many of the same techniques used to protect livestock can also be used to protect crops, including fencing, guard dogs, and the general repelling effect of human scent and activity.

Coyotes in Trash—Improper storage or exposure of trash can attract coyotes to an area. If practical, trash should be stored in the garage until the day of pickup. Secure, tightly-fitted lids are important for trash receptacles stored outdoors. A small volume of ammonia or pepper may discourage coyotes from scavenging in garbage cans.

Domestic Pets—Although coyote predation on domestic animals is uncommon, it may sometimes arise as a concern. Steps that can be taken to reduce threats include feeding and

PUBLIC HEALTH

TYPES OF DAMAGE

CONTROL METHODS

keeping pets indoors, removing cover and areas for concealment around homes, proper trash sanitation, and awareness and surveillance aimed at identifying threats before they become problems. Be aware of coyotes in an area and sensitive to the things attracting them there, then take steps to remove the sources of attraction.

DEER

Deer are even-toed ungulates, common and easily recognized as one of our largest mammals. The white-tailed deer is the most widely distributed species, occurring in all of the lower forty-eight states with the possible exception of Utah. Mule and black-tailed deer represent races of the western species. They share much of their range with white-tail deer.

NATURAL HISTORY

Habitat—Although deer are essentially a woodland species, they can adapt to a variety of habitats. Some cover is necessary, and deer prefer the low growth that is characteristic of newly-established woodlots.

Diet—Deer eat many different plant species, typically browsing on leaves, stems, and buds of woody plants and the fruits and seeds of many agricultural crops. Hard mast, such as acorns, is important for fattening in the fall. Feeding preferences vary greatly from one area to another.

Breeding—Breeding occurs from October to January, the time of onset varies, depending on the geographic area. Gestation is between 200 and 205 days, and from one to three fawns may be produced, depending on the general health and condition of the mother.

LEGAL STATUS

Deer are classified as game species, and they may be killed only during the open season by persons possessing valid hunting licenses. At other times of the year, deer are protected, and they may be killed or removed from property only under the conditions set by the game department. No special permit is required to deer-proof a premise.

Deer are important hosts of the ticks that carry Lyme disease. Also, statistics from the National Highway Administration indicate that approximately 8,000 people are injured each year in accidents between autos and wildlife. Deer are involved in a substantial number of these incidents.

Deer damage is usually not difficult to determine, as either the animals themselves, their tracks, or their droppings are observed. Where deer damage to plants could be confused with that inflicted by rabbits or rodents, look for a ragged, squared, torn appearance at the end of browsed twigs. Deer do not have upper incisors and do not neatly clip-browse as do other species. Where browsing occurs 3–5 feet from the ground, the damage is normally associated with deer. In areas heavily populated with deer, a browse line may develop. Vegetation will have a neat clipped appearance that extends up to 5 feet above ground. Deer feed extensively on branches, and small trees, such as elms, may be stripped of bark.

Exclusion—Where deer are a problem and the resource (crops, ornamental plantings) they threaten can be protected by fencing (see fig. 11), this is the most effective, permanent solution to damage. Several effective fence designs have been developed featuring high-tensile wiring, standard mesh designs, angled placement, and various types of electric wiring. The best type for any given area will depend on many considerations, and local extension specialists should be consulted about the best use of fencing.

Repellents—Repellents can be used effectively to keep deer from select orchard crops, vegetables, and ornamental plantings. Two general kinds of repellents are available: those that repel directly by taste and those that work indirectly and repel by smell, sight, or sound. A good example of taste repellents would be any of the variety of commercial preparations using thiram or other bittering agents. Commercial products such as Hinder or Deer-Away can repel by both smell and taste. Solutions are painted or sprayed onto tree trunks or foliage to be protected; the bitter taste and noxious smell cause avoidance shortly after deer attempt to feed. It is important to start treatments early, usually when plants first go dormant in the fall, and to continue with reapplications following manufacturer's recommendations. Area repellents include such varied methods as putting out old nylon stockings containing small amounts of human hair (see fig. 12) or hanging mirrors, tinfoil strips, or commercial repellants in places to be protected. Scarecrows and wind-generated noisemakers may also repel deer under appropriate circumstances. Effectiveness varies with any of these techniques, but in general it should be remembered that deer, like most animals, are adaptable and will soon adjust to and ignore any consistent non-harmful stimulus.

Trapping—In special cases, deer can be trapped live or tranquilized and relocated from areas in which severe damage occurs where they have strayed or been frightened. This must be done by experienced personnel, and it is advisable, before emergencies arise, that a team qualified to act be formed locally and to be on call to respond. Chemical immobilization is costly, requires special equipment, and must be conducted by trained (and often certified) personnel. Deer densities are high in many areas and suitable relocation sites for deer are often not available.

HOUSE MICE

The house mouse is a small, gray-brown rodent typically weighing less than 1 ounce, with an almost naked tail as long as, or longer than, its body and with large, pointed ears. Close relatives include the wild white-footed mouse, the deer mouse, and the meadow vole.

Habitat—House mice are *commensal*, which means literally "sharing the table." They prefer to live in structures and buildings provided by humans or close by human residences.

Diet—Mice are omnivores and eat a variety of foods, preferring seeds, grains, and nuts. Mice require only about $1/10$ ounce of food each day, and they can live without access to fresh water.

Breeding—House mice breed year-round and can raise as many as eight litters annually. Reproductive life begins for females at one and a half to two months of age. With an average of four to seven young per litter, the reproductive potential of these animals is considerable. House mice will live for about one year.

Mice are classified as unprotected species. They may be killed, captured, or otherwise controlled without special authorization from the state game department. The manner of control, however, must be safe and humane and must conform with any other applicable laws. Many of the products used in rodent control, such as poisons, are regulated under federal law.

PUBLIC HEALTH

Mice can transmit several diseases to humans, including salmonellosis, leptospirosis, and rat-bite fever. Particular care should be taken to avoid the consumption of food substances contaminated by mice.

TYPES OF DAMAGE

When present in large numbers, mice will consume large quantities of stored seed and grains. More damage to food substances is caused by contamination with urine and feces than by consumption, however. By gnawing wood, paper, cloth, books, and insulation from wiring, mice may also cause considerable property damage. Direct observation will indicate damage, as gnawing leaves tooth marks about $^1/_8$ inch wide. Nests may be found in hidden places such as assemblages of paper, cloth, and other material. Droppings are rod-shaped, about $^1/_8$ inch long, and the best indicator of the presence of mice in the house.

CONTROL METHODS

Exclusion—Mice can enter buildings through openings no larger than the size of a dime and can easily climb interior walls, making exclusion sometimes very difficult. Coarse steel wool or quick drying cement can be used to plug cracks around drain pipes and small openings where mice may gain access. Hardware cloth (¼ inch mesh or less) is effective in larger areas.

Habitat Modification—The removal of food sources through proper sanitary techniques is essential. Household food items that are accessible to mice should be stored in metal or plastic containers. Holes or cracks in exterior walls should be sealed to prevent animals from entering the premises. Outside, a protective cover can be eliminated by removing weeds and trimming around the base of shrubs that are planted next to the building. Pets should be fed indoors and uneaten food picked up where mice are known to be a problem. Spill trays on bird feeders will remove an attractive winter food source for both mice and rats.

Removal—A cage trap can be used to remove mice unharmed from inside buildings, but unless entryways are sealed and sources of food eliminated, other mice will be attracted to the premises.

MOLES

Moles are small mammals from 4–6 inches long, with eyes often hidden in fur, naked snouts, no external ears, and characteristic paddle-shaped, enlarged forelegs. Seven species occur in North America, with the eastern and the star-nosed species the most widely distributed.

NATURAL HISTORY

Habitat—Moles spend most of their lives underground and rarely make an appearance on the surface. They prefer moist, loose soils of the sort favored by the grubs and earthworms that are their main source of food.

Diet—Moles eat very few plants. Their diet consists primarily of insects and grubs. Where plant damage and mole tunnels are associated, it is usually because of rodents (mice and voles) using the tunnels, rather than from the mole itself.

Breeding—Breeding occurs in late

winter and early spring; litter size usually ranges from three to seven. The young are born in a deeper burrow than those normally seen on the surface and become active within the burrow runs at about four weeks of age.

LEGAL STATUS

In most states moles are classified as an unprotected species. Animals may be killed, captured, or otherwise controlled without special authorization from the state game department. The manner of control, however, must be safe and humane and must conform with any other applicable laws.

PUBLIC HEALTH

Moles are not considered to be a significant source for any infectious disease that can be transmitted to humans.

TYPES OF DAMAGE

Moles are often blamed for damage caused by other species. On golf courses and lawns, the evidence of mole presence is frequently seen in their excavations, either in small mounds of earth (molehills) resulting from deep tunneling, or shallow surface tunnels or runs that collapse underfoot and are a source of annoyance to some.

CONTROL METHODS

Since moles feed primarily on insects, grubs, and earthworms and aerate and loosen soil by tunneling, emphasis should first be placed on explaining their beneficial role. Prevention of moles in large areas can often be achieved by controlling the insect populations that are their major source of food. Grub-proofing lawns and the control of adult insects are likely to lead to reduced mole populations.

Exclusion—Barriers can be erected around small flower or garden plots by use of hardware cloth (¼ inch mesh) buried around the perimeter to a depth of 12 inches and placed so that approximately another 12 inches extend out at a 90 degree angle.

Repellents—Any of the variety of commercial repellents containing thiram can be used to protect bulbs from damage by rodents utilizing mole tunnels. Some success has been reported by using children's pinwheels or other devices, which are pushed into tunnels and transmit vibrations through the burrow. Commercial battery-operated devices are available that claim effectiveness over areas of 1,000 square yards. As with all such products and claims, the buyer should work with reputable marketing sources who guarantee return of costs if the product proves ineffective. One product that is a registered pesticide, but is not approved for use as a repellent of moles, is napthalene. Neither moth flakes nor moth balls can be used for the control of moles.

Trapping—Moles can be trapped live; however, relocation should be attempted only as a last resort since moles cannot live for more than a few hours without feeding. To live trap, a container such as a large coffee can is buried along currently used tunnels. The ends of the tunnel are collapsed in front of the can, and the mole is trapped after it digs through this obstruction. Traps must be monitored closely, and trapped animals must be removed and relocated quickly.

MUSKRATS

This dark brown, rabbit-sized rodent is well adapted to its aquatic life with large, partially webbed hind feet, a dense waterproof coat, and a long naked tail that is flattened from side to side to make an effective rudder.

NATURAL HISTORY

Habitat—Muskrats may be found in almost any body of water throughout their range, including drainage ditches, streams, ponds, lakes, fresh-water marshes, and brackish marshes. They live in lodges built of piled vegetation and mud or in burrows dug into the banks of streams and ponds. Muskrats are active all year.

Diet—Muskrats are primarily plant eaters and prefer to feed on aquatic plants such as cattails, bulrushes, and algae. They may occasionally eat small aquatic animals.

Breeding—Muskrats breed from April to August in the northern United States, as well as the winter in the deep south. An older female may produce three litters of five or six young per year. Local populations may occasionally increase to such densities that most of the marsh vegetation in the area is eaten or damaged. Such events are normally followed by a sharp decline in muskrat numbers.

LEGAL STATUS

Muskrats are classified as furbearers and may be killed only by licensed trappers during the open season established by the state game department. At other times of the year, muskrats are protected, and they may be killed or removed from property only under the conditions set by the game department. Animal-proofing may be performed at any time of the year without special permission from the game department.

Muskrats may be infected with tularemia, which may be transmitted to people through blood to blood contact or by eating inadequately cooked muskrat meat.

A muskrat burrow can threaten the structural integrity of a pond dam or dike. Evidence of their presence includes 5–6 inch diameter burrows in banks at or below the water level, emergent aquatic plants cut off at water level, or dome-shaped lodges made of mud and plants in shallow water.

Muskrat burrows are seldom a real threat to properly constructed dams that have an impermeable core and substantial thickness. The threat must also be weighed against the benefits muskrats provide by controlling algae and other aquatic weeds that can overwhelm small ponds.

Exclusion—Dams can be protected against muskrat burrowing by the placement of a continuous layer of riprap (stone) that extends from 2 feet below the normal water level to 2 feet above. A barrier can also be fashioned from welded wire, galvanized hardware cloth, or poultry netting buried along the same area.

Muskrats may be driven from existing burrows in dams by probing with a metal rod just above the burrow entrance to find the nest chamber and then digging down to expose it. The muskrats will leave immediately, and the burrow can then be filled in and a barrier installed. If babies are discovered in the burrow, stop digging but leave the burrow partially exposed. The mother will probably remove the babies to another burrow by the next day, and the burrow can then be filled and barricaded. Burrows not located directly in the dam should not be a problem.

Habitat Modification—It may be possible to discourage muskrats from taking up residence in a pond by controlling the aquatic plants on which they feed. This can be very difficult, however, since persistent herbicides should not be applied to water, and manual plant removal is hard work that must be ongoing to be effective.

Trapping—Muskrats can be live-trapped, but it is unlikely that all the members in a colony can be caught. Muskrats will readily enter a live-trap cage placed in the water just outside the burrow and baited with apples. It is important to set the trap in water shallow enough so the captured muskrat can breathe air. Check the trap frequently, and release the muskrat in a large body of water. Do not trap during the breeding season.

OPOSSUMS

The opossum is a medium-sized mammal about the size of a house cat, with coarse white/gray fur, naked ears, and a long, almost hairless tail. Depending on age, length may vary from 1–3 feet (with tail) and weight from less than 2 to over 10 pounds. Although they appear formidable and are often mistaken for large rats, opossums are shy and inoffensive animals.

NATURAL HISTORY

Habitat—The opossum is the only marsupial found in North America. It ranges over most of the east and midwestern states and in the far west along the Pacific Coast. Opossums occur in a variety of habitats but prefer deciduous woodlands. They can be common in urban and suburban areas.

Diet—Opossums are omnivores and

will eat a wide range of plant and animal foods and scavenge carrion and garbage when available.

Breeding—Birth is given to young, little more developed than embryos, which crawl into a pouch on the mother where they nurse and mature for about ten weeks. Females may breed twice a year, and litters can include as many as a dozen young. The young become independent of the mother at about three months of age.

LEGAL STATUS

In most states, the opossum is classified as a game species. Animals may be hunted and trapped during the game season established by a state game department. At other times of the year, opossums may be protected. They may be killed or removed from property only under the conditions set by the game department. Animal-proofing may be performed at any time of the year without special permission from the game department.

PUBLIC HEALTH

Opossums are susceptible to a variety of diseases of significance to humans, but their role in the transmission of any is uncertain. Rabies does occur in opossums but is rare.

TYPES OF DAMAGE

Opossums infrequently cause damage similar to skunks and raccoons by raiding garbage cans, damaging fruit and vegetable crops, and killing an occasional bird in a poultry yard. Overall, the level of damage caused by these animals is slight, and they are probably more beneficial as scavengers than harmful for any damage they cause.

CONTROL METHODS

Opossums can be kept out of structures by following the exclusion techniques used for skunks and raccoons. Since opossums tend to use ground dens, exclusion using one-way doors can be effective (see fig. 2). The most effective method of discouraging visits by an opossum is to secure trash containers with tight-fitting lids and pick up food at night if pets are fed outdoors.

Opossum in House—Occasionally opossums enter houses through pet doors. They generally can be coaxed out the way they came in, or the door may be left open for the opossum to find its way out.

PRAIRIE DOGS, POCKET GOPHERS, GROUND SQUIRRELS

Prairie dogs, pocket gophers, and ground squirrels are burrow-dwellers, represented by numerous species and occurring widely in the United States except in the mid-Atlantic and northeastern states. The term "gopher" may be applied locally to any species, and consultation with wildlife specialists may be necessary for exact identification of species where damage occurs. These are all medium-sized rodents, ranging from 5 inches in length in the smaller pocket gophers to more than 1 foot in some ground squirrels and prairie dogs. Coat color varies widely but generally is brownish with lighter and darker variants.

NATURAL HISTORY

Habitat—Pocket gophers occur in the widest variety of habitats of the animals discussed here, ranging from low areas along the southeastern coast to inland areas of high elevation. Prairie dogs prefer more extensive grasslands, and the different ground squirrels range from open grassland to wooded areas. Friable soils suitable for burrowing are important if any of these species are to be abundant.

Diet—All of the animals described in this section are heavy utilizers of plant material, most notably grasses and forbs. Some of the ground squirrels will utilize a variety of plant materials including mast, and pocket gophers will eat bark from shrubs and trees.

LEGAL STATUS

Most of these animals are classified as unprotected species under state wildlife laws. They may be killed, captured, or otherwise controlled without special authorization from the state game department. The manner of control, however, must conform with any other applicable laws. In particular, the poisons and fumigants commonly used to control these animals are regulated under federal law.

PUBLIC HEALTH

The animals discussed in this section generally are not considered to be a significant source for any infectious disease that can be transmitted to humans, with the notable exception of the role played by ground squirrels in transmitting plague.

TYPES OF DAMAGE

Agricultural crops, pasture, and occasional garden crops are damaged. Signs of burrowing, such as mounds of earth at entrances, and observation of the animals themselves are helpful where ground squirrel or prairie dog damage occurs. Pocket gophers live almost entirely underground, but the extensive burrowing, numerous mounds of excavated earth, and plugging of burrow entrances with earth or grass, are indicators of their presence.

CONTROL METHODS

The most serious damage caused is in agricultural areas, and consultation with extension specialists and the development of a management plan is recommended there. Crop rotation and alternate plantings may help control pocket gopher problems in some areas. As always, identification of the species causing the problem and an understanding of its natural history is critical. The development of an integrated management plan, with the long-term goal of reducing damage to acceptable levels while avoiding the need for repeated suppression of population, is a key to dealing with problems caused by the species discussed here.

Around Homes—Fencing is generally not practical as a means of excluding any of these animals except in special cases. Hardware cloth (¼ or ½ inch mesh) can be placed to a depth of 18–20 inches around small plots of individual ornamental plants and trees, or trunks can be wrapped in commercial tree wrap (see fig. 4). Habitat modification practices aimed at reducing cover, controlling weeds, and limiting available forage may be successful. Some success in controlling pocket gophers may be achieved by keeping lawns irrigated and constantly moist, creating an unsuitable soil structure for burrow maintenance. A specialized application of fencing in a municipal ballpark involved the horizontal application of woven wire mesh over an entire playing surface, which was then covered by soil. This method illustrates the imaginative thinking that can be applied to conflicts between people and wildlife.

COTTONTAIL RABBITS

Cottontails and their close relatives include eight species in the United States, with the eastern cottontail being the most widespread and familiar. All are grayish or brownish, have large ears and hind feet, and short, fluffy tails. They are smaller and have shorter limbs than their cousins, the hares and jackrabbits.

This section refers primarily to the eastern cottontail, which is most commonly involved in rabbit pest situations.

Habitat—Cottontails are generally found in brushy hedgerows and wood edges with dense cover, but they also do very well in suburbs and urban areas with lawns, gardens, and shrubs.

Diet—Rabbits feed on leafy plants during the growing season and the buds and bark of woody plants in the winter. They are most active from dusk to dawn.

Breeding—Famous for their reproductive abilities, cottontails breed from February through September, producing three or four litters of four or five young per year. Young are born helpless in a shallow depression lined with grass and mother's fur, but they grow rapidly and are weaned when less than half the size of the adult. Cottontails are preyed upon by many predators and seldom live more than one year in the wild. Where natural predators are present, rabbits may rarely be seen during the day.

NATURAL HISTORY

LEGAL STATUS

Rabbits are classified as game animals. Animals are hunted and trapped during the open season established by a state game department. At other times of the year rabbits are protected, and they may be killed or removed from property only under the conditions set by the game department. Animal-proofing may be performed at any time of the year without special permission from the game department.

PUBLIC HEALTH

Rabbits are occasionally infected with tularemia, which may be transmitted to people if they eat undercooked, infected meat, handle a sick animal, or allow an open cut to contact the infected meat of a butchered rabbit. Rabbits are more likely to be infected in warm weather and mild climates.

Cottontail damage is principally a result of their feeding activities. In the spring and summer, they may damage flower and vegetable beds. In the fall and winter, they will eat the bark of fruit trees and ornamentals, occasionally girdling and killing the plant. Damage may be distinguished from other animals by the cleanly cut plant remains and the presence of nearly spherical droppings scattered around the area. Their easily recognizable tracks may also be found in soft soil or snow.

Protecting Flowers and Vegetables—The most effective, permanent protection of gardens subject to rabbit damage is a well-constructed fence. The fence normally needs to be only 2 feet high and made of 1 inch poultry wire stretched between posts, with the lower edge staked securely to the ground or slightly buried to prevent passage under the fence. Most garden plants are only likely to be eaten as young shoots, so the fence may be moved as the plants mature. It may be more practical to fence the perimeter of a small suburban lot rather than each individual garden bed.

If fencing is impractical, small plots and individual plants may be protected with chemical repellents that rabbits find distasteful. Commercial repellents are available in most garden centers and nurseries. These will have to be applied repeatedly as the plants grow and usually should not be used on vegetables once the edible parts begin to develop.

Protecting Trees and Shrubs—
Barriers such as commercial tree wrap
(see fig. 4) may be effective at preventing bark damage by rabbits. Perhaps
more reliable are guards made of
cylinders of hardware cloth, which are
more self-supporting, or poultry wire,
which would require more staking.
These barriers are placed around the
trunks to a height equal to the expected
snow depth plus 18 inches. Young trees
and saplings are more vulnerable than
old trees with thicker, tougher bark.
Low hanging branches may also be
within reach of rabbits and should be
included inside the barrier if possible.
Routine pruning done in the fall will
provide a decoy food source for the rabbits if trimmings are left on the ground.
Rabbits find twigs and buds more
desirable than trunk bark and will concentrate their feeding on these.

Chemical repellents are also available
for protecting woody plants from rabbit damage. Check local nurseries for
commercial repellents. These usually
only require one application in the fall
for the entire dormant season. Follow
the label directions carefully.

Habitat Modification—Rabbits avoid
areas with little cover because of the
danger from natural predators. For this
reason, mowing lawns around gardens
and orchards will help reduce damage.
It is also useful to attract natural rabbit
predators such as hawks and owls.

Trapping Rabbits—Live trapping and
relocating rabbits to reduce damage
may only be considered a temporary
solution at best, since relocated rabbits
will soon be replaced by reproduction
and immigration, so it is not recommended. If trapping is done, the trap
should be set in a sheltered spot and

baited with apples. Trapped rabbits should be released in suitable habitat as soon as possible to avoid self-inflicted injuries.

RACCOONS

The raccoon is easily recognized by its dark facial mask and ringed tail. Length varies from 1½–2½ feet, with males tending to be larger than females. Neither sex typically exceeds 25 pounds. By nature shy, raccoons may become bold once familiar with and conditioned to people. Raccoons are at least as intelligent as cats or dogs and possess far greater manual dexterity.

Habitat—Although they prefer mature woodlands, raccoons are adaptable animals and can be found in most other habitats, ranging from seashore to prairie grasslands. Raccoons can live in close proximity to humans and are common in urban and suburban areas. Dens will be made above ground in tree cavities, chimneys, and attics, underground in old woodchuck burrows, storm sewers, and crawl spaces, and occasionally in odd places such as brush piles or old squirrel nests. While they are mostly active at night (nocturnal), raccoons are sometimes active by day.

Diet—The raccoon's diet is highly varied and includes fruits, vegetables, nuts, insects, and small animals such as birds, amphibians, and mice. Fleshy fruits such as grapes and vegetables such as corn are preferred, and raccoons may be problems when competing for these and other foods raised by humans.

Breeding—Mating takes place from January to April, and births from March to June. Mating and birth seasons tend to come early in more northern latitudes and late further south. Occasional late births may occur in mid-summer to early fall. Litter size ranges from one to seven, with three to five usual. Young are weaned at about two months of age but usually remain with the mother through the first winter. The travel and exploratory activities of young, dispersing from the area in which they were born, often lead to conflicts with people.

LEGAL STATUS

Raccoons are classified as furbearing animals under state wildlife laws. Animals can be hunted and trapped during the game season established by a state fish and game department. At other times of the year, raccoons are protected, and they may be killed or removed from property only under the conditions set by the game department. Raccoon-proofing may be performed at any time of the year without special permission from the game department.

PUBLIC HEALTH

The raccoon is one of four wild animals considered to be primary carriers of the rabies virus. Currently, raccoon rabies is epidemic in the mid-Atlantic region of the United States. The raccoon roundworm (*Baylisacaris procyonis*) can infect humans who accidentally ingest or inhale its eggs, usually through contact with raccoon feces.

TYPES OF DAMAGE

Raccoons are often blamed for more damage than they cause, as when dogs or crows scatter trash from garbage cans that raccoons have opened. Where vegetable or fruit crops are being damaged, an attempt should be made to identify tracks. Raccoon presence in an attic or chimney is indicated by activity at dusk and just before dawn and often by noisy vocal exchanges. Since even mice can make considerable amounts of noise in walls or ceilings, it is important to verify that raccoons have taken up residence in a building. Raccoons using a house or other building will often deposit their feces in one particular place, a raccoon "latrine." These large, 3–6 inch, blunt scats often contain numerous plant seeds.

The *only* long-term, permanent means of coping with troublesome raccoons is to exclude animals from areas where they are unwanted. If raccoons are raiding garbage containers, they often can be repelled either by securing the garbage inside a can with a tight-fitting lid or by coating the garbage with a foul-smelling or foul-tasting item such as pepper. Removal of offending individuals by live trapping should be used only as a last resort and always followed by other measures to ensure there is no recurrence of the problem.

Raccoons in Chimneys—Raccoons will use uncapped chimneys for denning, and sometimes even giving birth and raising young in them. The fireplace flue, because of the smoke shelf, is usually the one used. Prevention is the first defense; chimney caps should be placed to prevent access by raccoons or other animals before they move in. Once a problem occurs, efforts should be made to exclude the raccoon, ensure no young remain behind, and prevent further access. Raccoons do not tolerate strong odors, and napthalene or ammonia can sometimes be used to drive them from chimneys. From above, a bag filled with moth balls or rags soaked in ammonia can be lowered by rope and left in the chimney until raccoons have departed. If the fireplace opening has glass doors or can otherwise be sealed, a dish of ammonia can be placed so that the smell is carried upward by chimney drafts. Care should be taken at all times to ensure that cubs too young to climb are not left in the chimney. Raccoons always have alternate den sites to which they will move if disturbed, and the mother will move her young if given a chance.

Raccoons in Attics—The attic should be inspected to determine where access is occurring, and the opening should be sealed once the raccoon is evicted or leaves the premises. Usually, attics are too large to use odor repellents, but increased activity, turning lights on, and leaving a portable radio on for one or two days will create enough disturbance to cause the raccoon to leave. An examination of the exterior of the house will often show a tree limb overhanging the roof and providing access. It is advisable to trim such limbs back from the house.

Raccoons in Houses—Occasionally raccoons will enter a house through a pet door and be unable to find their way out. Since they can cause considerable damage when panicked, it is advisable to withdraw, open windows and doors through which the raccoon could exit, close doors providing access to other parts of the house, and wait quietly for the animal to make its escape. The capture and handling of live raccoons should be attempted only by professionals.

Raccoons in Trash—Raccoons often defeat even the most apparently secure trash systems and, once accustomed to finding a meal, will return again and again. If trash can be stored inside a garage or shed where the animals have no access, they will quickly give up visits to the area. Straps, rubber "tie-downs," or weights on lids often discourage visits to the area. Using secure, tight-fitting lids and preventing cans from being overfilled are advisable. In some situations where assaults cannot otherwise be stopped, an inch or so of ammonia in the bottom of a can will quickly discourage further visits.

Raccoons in Gardens—Raccoons often cause considerable damage to garden fruits and vegetables, such as grapes and corn. Attacks often occur just before foods are ready to be picked, so extra vigilance at these times, chasing animals away, and using lights or radios to create disturbances may drive them away long enough to harvest the crop.

Trapping—As a last resort, individual raccoons that are responsible for chronic and repeated problems can be live-trapped and relocated. In some states this is now prohibited by law, while in others it is regulated under permit, so local fish and wildlife officials should be contacted before trapping is done. Removals should not be made between October and March except where mild climates allow, and extreme care should be taken to ensure that females raising young are not moved.

RATS

Rats are large, stocky rodents with an average weight of about 1 pound, small eyes and ears, grayish to dark brown fur, and naked tails. The nonnative Norway rat has become established almost everywhere, while the roof or black rat is restricted to the southern, southeastern, and western United States. Roof rats are more slender than Norway rats, have more pointed muzzles, and have tails that are longer than head and body combined.

NATURAL HISTORY

Habitat—Norway rats are found almost everywhere humans are but are most common in older, densely settled urban and suburban areas where reliable shelter and food are to be found. Norway rats will live in buildings but prefer to live in burrows dug along foundations or fence lines, under sidewalks, or in rocky debris piles. Roof rats tend to climb more than Norway rats, although they are perfectly capable of living on the ground.

Diet—Rats will eat a wide range of plant and animal foods. Adults require about 1 ounce of food a day. In the winter, seed spilled from bird feeders can be an important source of food. At all times refuse is freely consumed.

Breeding—Rats breed year-round, although peaks occur during the spring and fall. Breeding age is reached at two to three months, and litter size averages eight to twelve. One female can wean about twenty young a year.

LEGAL STATUS

Norway and roof rats are classified as unprotected species. Animals may be killed, captured, or otherwise controlled without special authorization from the state game department. The manner of control, however, must be safe and humane and must conform with any other applicable laws.

PUBLIC HEALTH

Rats are implicated in the transmission of a number of diseases to humans, and rat bites are a special concern. All bites that break the skin should be thoroughly washed with soap and water, and the victim should consult his or her personal physician.

TYPES OF DAMAGE

Rats damage food products through consumption and contamination with urine and feces, and they cause structural damage by their burrowing and gnawing. The presence of rats will be evident from their droppings, which are approximately ½ inch long and ¼ inch in diameter; their runs and burrows, which are obvious where populations are high; smudge or grease marks on walls or pipes where rats have travel routes in structures; and signs of gnawing on doors, in corners, or at points of access into buildings. In heavy infestations, rats are often heard in walls and attics or observed during daylight hours.

CONTROL METHODS

Exclusion—Rats can access buildings through holes no larger than ½ inch wide. All holes and openings should be sealed with heavy-weight material (¼ inch hardware cloth or better). Heating vents often are overlooked as points of entry, but they should be checked to ensure that access through them by rats is not possible. Outside, burrowing can be prevented along foundations by hardware cloth or concrete footers that are buried 12 inches and extend at 90 degrees another 12 inches from that (see fig. 13).

Habitat Modification—Proper sanitary techniques are not only essential but constitute the most economic and effective method to limiting rat presence. Tall grass should be mowed, and debris around building foundations should be removed. Food products should be stored in rat-proof containers. Refuse and garbage should be disposed of properly and stored where rats cannot gain access to them. Pet food should not be left outside. Old woodpiles are frequent havens for rats and should be removed.

Trapping—As with mice, under some circumstances rats can be trapped live and removed from an area. Care should be taken to avoid being bitten in such efforts, and, as always with any trapping program, other management activities should follow to ensure that problems do not recur.

Four species of skunks occur in the United States: spotted, striped, hooded, and hognose. Of these, the first two are widespread and the last two confined to the extreme southwest. All species are cat-size or smaller, have long fur, long bushy tails, and are black and white. They are well known for their ability to defend themselves with extremely pungent spray from specially adapted anal glands that are operational even in newborns.

The different species have similar habits; all are considered beneficial. Skunks are primarily nocturnal, good diggers, and eat mostly insects, but they will also eat mice, eggs, other small animals, and fruits. Skunks are usually solitary with the exception of a mother with her offspring, which she readily defends. Skunks are known for their slow, waddling gait and apparent fearlessness, which is largely justified since most predators know enough to leave them alone. They are active all year except during the coldest spells in the northern states, when they hibernate. Five to ten young are born around early May and remain in the burrow for about two months, after which they follow their mother single file as she forages. Skunks usually den in abandoned groundhog burrows, hollow logs, wood or rock piles, or under buildings. A den may only be used for brief periods before the skunk switches to another den.

SKUNKS

NATURAL HISTORY

LEGAL STATUS

Skunks are classified as furbearers under most state wildlife laws. These animals can be trapped with a license during the open season established by a state fish and game department. At other times of the year, skunks are normally protected and can be killed or removed from property only under the conditions set by the game department. Skunk-proofing may be performed at any time of the year without special permission from the game department.

PUBLIC HEALTH

Skunks sometimes carry rabies. Skunk spray in eyes is extremely irritating and may cause temporary blindness, but no permanent damage will result.

TYPES OF DAMAGE

Skunks are usually smelled before they are seen. Odor may linger for days in the area where a skunk has sprayed. Persistent, faint skunk odor associated with a 4–6 inch diameter hole under a building or woodpile indicates that a skunk has taken up residence. While foraging for grubs, skunks may dig many shallow holes in a lawn. Look for long black or white hairs or a faint odor to confirm that some other animal is not responsible for these holes. Skunks will be attracted to garbage or pet food left out at night. They occasionally raid chicken houses for eggs or young chickens. Skunks may also become trapped in window wells and discovered by an unfortunate person or pet. Naive dogs and cats will be sprayed if they harass a skunk.

CONTROL METHODS

Habitat Modification—Occasional skunk sightings in a neighborhood need not be cause for alarm, since they are common in the right habitat. It would be impractical and even undesirable to remove them from a large area. Preventive measures such as removing attractants from the vicinity of houses will decrease the likelihood of an unpleasant encounter. Attractants include garbage and pet food left out at night and convenient denning sites such as wood and rock piles, elevated sheds, openings under concrete slabs and porches, and access to crawl spaces under houses. Openings in buildings should be closed up with boards or screening that extend 8–10 inches underground. Openings under concrete structures should be backfilled with dirt, and debris piles should be removed or stacked neatly to eliminate suitable cavities.

Check for Activity—Discovery of a den suspected to harbor a skunk should first be checked to determine if it is currently occupied. This may be done by covering the hole (or holes) with loose dirt. If a skunk is present, it will easily dig its way out that night and reopen the hole. If the dirt remains undisturbed for two or three nights (and it is not winter), it may be assumed that the hole is unoccupied and it may be permanently closed with masonry, boards, or hardware cloth.

Evicting the Skunk—A skunk may be evicted from an active den by installing a one-way door over the entrance that allows the skunk to leave but prevents reentry (see fig. 2). Care must be taken to ensure that the door can open without hitting an obstruction. Leave the door in place for two or three nights to be sure that the skunk has left. Be sure that no new holes appear nearby. Remove the door and close the opening as described above. *Caution:* Do not install a one-way door in May or June when there may be babies left behind in the den. The babies may starve and possibly cause an odor problem. Instead, continue to place loose dirt over the hole until the skunk abandons the den due to the harassment. A mother skunk will carry her babies to a new den. Do not seal the opening until the dirt remains undisturbed for several nights.

Skunk in Chicken Coop—The only long-term control of skunk predation on chickens or eggs is to securely enclose the chickens in the coop at night. All openings must be repaired, and fencing around the coop should be extended 6–8 inches under ground to prevent skunks from digging under the fence.

Skunk in Window Well—If a skunk becomes trapped in a window well, the best method of freeing the animal is to provide it with a means of escape. Place a rough board (or one with cleats) in the well that is long enough to act as a ramp to the top. The board should lean no more steeply than a 45 degree angle. The board should be slowly and carefully placed by approaching the well low enough to be out of sight of the skunk. If possible, a second person with a vantage point high enough to see the skunk can warn of any signs of the skunk becoming agitated, such as raising its tail or stamping its forefeet. If this happens, the people should retreat immediately. Another method of placing the board is to tie it to the end of a long pole and lower it by holding the opposite end of the pole. Once the board is placed, keep people and pets away from the area until nightfall, when the skunk should leave on its own. To prevent this situation from recurring, place exit ramps or tight-fitting covers at each window well.

Deodorizing Pets and Property— Skunk odor on pets may be neutralized with liberal amounts of vinegar or tomato juice. This will make the odor tolerable—only time will eliminate it. Chlorine bleach, ammonia, or commercial products containing neutroleum alpha may be used on inanimate objects. Carbolic soap and water are safe to use on skin. Liberal flushing with cold water will ease the discomfort of skunk spray in the eyes.

Trapping—Use of the techniques described above usually makes trapping unnecessary. However, if there is no alternative, skunks may be captured in box traps baited with cat food or tuna fish. Wooden traps are preferred over wire cage traps because they offer a barrier against getting sprayed by the trapped skunk. A skunk in a dark, covered trap will usually remain calm if handled carefully. Wire traps should be partially covered with a tarp or burlap when they are set. If confronted with a skunk in an uncovered wire trap, approach it slowly with a tarp held up in front as a shield; the tarp will eventually be used to cover the trap. Watch for signs that the skunk is agitated and back away until it calms down again. The skunk should be transported at least 10 miles away and released in suitable habitat.

SNAKES

There are about 250 species and subspecies of snakes in the United States, each with its own distinct markings, life history, and habitat requirements. Snakes are rarely encountered by people. Of those snakes that share human habitats, most are harmless. For the purposes of animal-damage control, as well as human safety, it is important to distinguish between venomous and nonvenomous snakes. There are four types of poisonous snakes in the United

States: the copperhead, the coral snake, the rattlesnake, and the water moccasin. It is strongly recommended that an appropriate field guide or other authority be consulted to learn which poisonous and common nonpoisonous snakes occur in an area and for identification of particular animals. Wide-ranging types of snakes most commonly encountered by people include garter snakes, rat snakes, water snakes, hog-nosed snakes, milk snakes, and ringneck snakes. None of these common snakes is poisonous, and they perform a beneficial role by consuming small rodents.

NATURAL HISTORY

Habitat—Each species has its unique natural history and habitat requirements. The snakes that people are likely to encounter are those which frequent gardens, farms, and suburban habitats. Snakes are usually secretive and retreat from threats if given a chance. They cannot hear sounds and are nearsighted, but they are very sensitive to vibrations on the ground and have a good sense of smell (they flick their tongues to gather odors from the air). Snakes cannot dig holes in firm soil, but they will readily use an available opening such as a mouse hole.

LEGAL STATUS

In most states snakes are classified as protected nongame species under the wildlife laws. A nonpoisonous snake may not be harmed except under the special conditions set by the game department. The regulations governing the control of snakes can be obtained from a local game warden.

PUBLIC HEALTH

Snakes are not known to transmit any disease to humans. Nonpoisonous snake bites that break the skin should be treated like any puncture wound with a potential for infection. Victims of poisonous bites should stay calm and inactive, if possible, and should seek a doctor immediately. Physicians now urge people not to administer first aid for a snakebite since most procedures do more harm than good.

Snakes do not cause property damage. Their presence is usually discovered when a person happens upon an animal, its shed skin, or its droppings, which are usually black and white and resemble bird droppings.

Snakes in houses fall into two categories: those that entered accidentally and want to escape what to them is unsuitable habitat; and those that have entered to find prey or shelter and would take up permanent residence if allowed. The former category includes most of the very small snakes, like young garter snakes and ringneck snakes that may be considered trapped in the house and will likely die from lack of food or moisture if not captured and removed.

Snakes that may become residents include rat snakes, king snakes, black snakes, and other rodent-eating species that often follow mouse trails into buildings, or any other snake large enough to climb around freely inside the walls and between floors. Some snakes may hibernate in older houses with leaky cellars or crawl spaces with dirt floors. The presence of shed skins usually indicates that a snake has been living in the house for some time, coming and going at will.

Snakes in the Yard—There is usually no reason to be alarmed by a snake in the yard unless it is determined to be poisonous. Its presence indicates that there is appropriate habitat available, and it may have lived nearby for years without being observed by a human. If left alone, the snake may never be encountered again. If it is suspected to be poisonous, it should be given wide berth, and an expert snake handler should be called to identify the species and remove it if necessary. An adult should be assigned to watch its movements from a safe distance while the expert is summoned. Many snake bites occur when an inexperienced person tries to catch or kill a snake. Moreover, most of the snakes killed by people are later identified as harmless species.

A homeowner may minimize the chance of a snake taking up residence in the yard by making the area unattractive to it. This means removing potential hiding places for snakes and their prey, which include piles of rocks, wood, or other debris, tall grass and undergrowth, cracks around concrete porches and sidewalks, and storage sheds with space under the floor. Pet foods and household garbage left unprotected outside overnight attract rodents, and, in turn, the presence of rats or mice may attract snakes. Grounds that are manicured and kept free of debris generally make poor snake habitat.

It is possible to construct a snake-proof fence around a yard out of ¼ inch mesh hardware cloth that is buried 2 inches at the base, angled outward approximately 30 degrees, and 3 feet high. Gates have to seal tightly if the fence is to be truly snake-proof. The expense of such a fence is seldom justified, however.

Snake in the House—When a snake is discovered in a house, remain calm and avoid any act that might disturb it and drive it into hiding. It may be possible to carefully open a nearby door and use a broom to gently, but quickly, herd it out. Or, it may be possible to place an empty pail or wastebasket slowly over a small or coiled snake and then put a weight on it to trap the snake until an experienced handler can come to remove it. If the snake can be confined in a room or corner with barriers such as boards or boxes, it will be available to be captured when the expert arrives. Captured snakes should be released in natural areas more than 1 mile away, during warm weather. Once the snake has been captured or has escaped, the homeowner can proceed to snake-proof the property.

Snakes usually enter a premises at ground level, perhaps through a tiny crack or hole no more than $1/8$ inch wide. An intensive inspection of the foundation for unsealed wire or pipe conduits or basement windows or doors that do not seal tightly will usually reveal the snake entrance. All such openings should be sealed immediately.

Residents—These snakes may be extremely difficult to locate and capture, even by an expert, since they are capable of retreating for long periods (weeks) inside walls or in other inaccessible locations in the building. Also, there may be more than one snake inhabiting the same house, so capture and removal of one may not solve the problem.

After the discovery of a snake in a house, the entire house should be inspected inside and outside to evaluate the situation. The interior inspection should be concentrated on the basement and first floor, but check the attic also because larger snakes will often climb inside the walls and emerge in an unfinished attic. The purpose of the inspection is not only to look for snakes, but also for potential openings that allow snakes entry into rooms. These include any openings in the walls and floor, such as unsealed wire and pipe penetrations or unfinished closets. If there is reason to believe that a snake could enter a room, check under and behind furniture, appliances, boxes, and piles of clothes for a concealed snake. These interior openings may be sealed upon discovery with appropriate materials.

Next, inspect the house exterior for possible entrances, particularly at or near ground level. Keep in mind the size of the snake that was discovered and look for any opening large enough for the snake's head to pass through. Many snakes are also good climbers, so check for plantings that may give access to the roof. A fieldstone wall or chimney may also be climbable by a snake. If such access is present, check for openings around the eaves and roof. Another common place of entry is behind concrete porches or steps or where decks attach to the house. Sometimes these openings are very difficult to locate, and it may seem like none exist, but keep in mind that the snake had to get in somehow.

Once the entire exterior has been inspected and one or more openings have been discovered, decide which opening is likely to be the main snake entrance. To determine the snake's route of travel, consider the size of the openings, ease of access by the snake, and clear penetration into the area of the house where the snake was discovered. Seal all the openings except the main snake entrance. Attach a one-way door to the remaining entrance. This may be a tube made from rolled window screen that, when properly installed, will allow any snakes remaining inside to get out but not re-enter. It may be left in place for a month or longer to allow time for the snake to leave. If it is fall when the door is installed, leave it in place until well into the following spring. After removing the door, permanently seal the opening. It may not be possible to completely snake-proof an old house, particularly if mice have built an elaborate system of tunnels into the basement.

EASTERN GRAY SQUIRRELS

The eastern gray squirrel is a 16–20 inch (including bushy tail half its total length) rodent, usually gray or brownish-gray on sides and back and whitish below, but occasionally all black. Close relatives of the eastern gray squirrel, including the western gray and eastern fox squirrel, have very similar life histories and may cause similar problems with the same solutions as discussed here. Southern flying squirrels may also nest in buildings on wooded sites and may be excluded using the same techniques as for other squirrels. Flying squirrels are strictly nocturnal, may share a den with up to twenty other adults (particularly in winter), and breed twice a year as described below for the gray squirrel.

Habitat—Never found far from trees, the eastern gray squirrel is from the eastern deciduous forest and has adapted to our landscaped suburbs and urban parks, reaching its highest con-

NATURAL HISTORY

centrations where oaks and hickories dominate or where people supply food in bird feeders or other sources. Dens may be in tree (or artificial) cavities or leaf nests in the branches of a tree.

Diet—Acorns and other nuts, fruits, tree buds, fungi, flower bulbs, and occasional bird eggs or nestlings.

Breeding—Usually two breeding seasons per year in late winter to early spring, and midsummer to early fall. Courtship is characterized by frantic male-female chases, often with several males pursuing one female. After mating, the female drives the males away and raises the two to five young (born about six weeks later) by herself. The babies are born naked and helpless and do not venture out of the nest for about seven or eight weeks. They are weaned at ten to twelve weeks. The spring litter is usually driven away by the mother shortly after weaning and as the next breeding cycle begins. The fall litter may stay with the mother in the nest through the winter until the next year's courtship season.

LEGAL STATUS

Most tree squirrels are classified as game animals under state wildlife laws. One subspecies of squirrel is protected under federal law as an endangered species. Animals are hunted and trapped during the open season established by a state game department. At other times of the year squirrels are protected, and they may legally be killed or removed from property only under the conditions set by the game department. Animal-proofing may be performed at any time of the year without special permission from the game department.

PUBLIC HEALTH

As mammals, squirrels may contract rabies, but only very rarely.

Most serious problems with squirrels involve adult females entering a building to establish a nest. They will explore any likely-looking opening while searching for a den site, and they often enter chimneys or attics through unscreened vents or openings left by loose or rotten boards. They invariably enter a building somewhere high on the structure and exploit an existing hole, though they may enlarge the hole by gnawing. A homeowner's first sign of the squirrel's presence is usually the sound of scampering in the attic or above the fireplace.

Squirrels entering chimneys are often unable to climb back out and, if possible, may emerge from a fireplace or follow a stovepipe to the furnace and emerge in the basement, whereupon they will attempt to get back outside. A squirrel found inside the living area of a house probably entered in this way and will instinctively seek windows trying to escape. In frustration, a squirrel can do a surprising amount of damage to window sills and adjacent furniture by gnawing on them.

Squirrels nesting in attics will usually gather insulation into a nest near the entrance and may gnaw on adjacent boards and electrical wires. Droppings may be scattered around the nest; they are dry, dark, and cylindrical, from ¼ – ½ inch long and about ⅛ inch in diameter.

Squirrels often become nuisances at bird feeders where they remove large quantities of bird seed and chew into feeders. Squirrels can also damage ornamental plants or fruit and nut trees by feeding on bark, buds, and fruits.

Nest in Attic—Thoroughly inspect inside the attic to find where the opening(s) is, where the nest is, and whether there are any babies present. Concentrate the search in the area where noises were heard. If there is no access to the attic, inspect the outside of the eaves, vents, and roof until the opening is located.

If the nest can be seen and there are no immature squirrels, attempt to frighten the squirrel outside by banging on the rafters inside the attic, or wait until you are sure all squirrels have left as they usually do during the day. Then seal up the opening with ½ inch mesh hardware cloth or sheet metal flashing, securely fastened. Extend the metal patch at least 6 inches beyond the hole in all directions to prevent the squirrel from gnawing around the patch. Seal any other weak spots or potential entrances in the same way. Listen carefully for the next day or so to be sure no squirrel was trapped inside or has regained entry.

If, for any reason, it cannot be determined if the squirrels are outside, do not seal the entrance. Instead, install a one-way door (see fig. 2), and leave it in place until no more sounds are heard inside the attic for several days. The door can then be removed and the opening patched as described above.

If the nest is inaccessible or out of sight, and there is the likelihood of babies (the squirrel has been in the house for more than a couple of days, and it is March through May or August through October), wait until the young have grown and have been observed coming out on their own. At that point, a one-way door may be installed over the opening, and left in place until no more sounds are heard inside the attic for several days. The door can then be removed and the opening patched.

Squirrel in Chimney (with fireplace)—It can be assumed that the squirrel is trapped in the chimney unless there is clear evidence it is able to climb out of the chimney on its own, either through direct observation or the presence of nesting material or babies. Do not try to smoke a squirrel out of a chimney—a trapped squirrel or babies may be killed and would then be very difficult to remove. If the squirrel is not trapped, proceed the same as with a nest in the attic as described above.

If the squirrel is above, or has access to, the flue damper, a means of escape may be provided by hanging a ½ inch thick rope down the chimney. Be sure to tie one end of the rope to the top of the chimney before lowering the other end, and make certain that it reaches the damper or smoke shelf. If a rope is unavailable, a series of boards or sticks may be securely attached end-to-end to sufficient length and substituted. Be careful not to lower anything into the chimney that cannot be easily retrieved. The squirrel will climb up the rope and escape, usually within a few (daylight) hours. After it is certain that the squirrel has escaped, remove the rope, and screen the chimney with ½ inch mesh hardware cloth or a commercially made cap.

If a squirrel is down in the fireplace (presumably behind the fireplace doors or screen), try tapping on the door and scaring it back up to above the damper. If successful, close the damper and proceed as above. If the squirrel cannot or will not leave the fireplace, the next best option is to obtain a suitable live trap, bait it with peanut butter, and set it very carefully inside the fireplace. Normally, the squirrel will retreat to a back corner of the fireplace as the doors are opened and stay there if the trap is placed, slowly and quietly, just inside the doors. Close the doors and wait quietly for the squirrel to enter the trap. As a precaution, before opening the doors of the fireplace to set the trap, close any interior doors in the room and open an exterior door or window in line of sight from the fireplace. In the event that the squirrel gets out of the fireplace, do not chase it; just sit quietly, and it will instinctively head for the light of the open door and go outside. After the squirrel has been removed, screen the chimney as described above.

Squirrel Loose in House—A squirrel that has entered a house has done so by accident and does not want to be there. If its exact location is known, close interior doors to limit its movement and open a window or exterior door in the room. The squirrel will find the opening if it is left alone, and it will even readily jump from a second story window without harming itself. If for some reason it is not possible to give the squirrel an exit, set a baited live-trap on the floor near the squirrel and leave it alone for at least a few hours. Once it has escaped or been captured, it is important to discover how it got in the house and prevent it from happening again. Look for tracks in soot or dust around the fireplace or furnace that may indicate that it came down the chimney, and check the attic for evidence of a nest or entrance hole that may need attention.

Raids on Bird Feeders—The agility of squirrels makes it difficult to prevent them from reaching bird feeders. Various devices have been designed to "baffle" squirrels, but none is foolproof. A comprehensive review of these devices may be found in *The Audubon Society Guide to Attracting Birds*, by Stephen W. Kress (1985, Charles Scribner's Sons, New York).

The best way to keep squirrels from becoming a problem at bird feeders is to prevent them from getting to the feeder in the first place. Once a squirrel becomes accustomed to feasting at a feeder, it will persistently try to overcome any obstacles that are placed in its way.

Squirrels can be deterred from pilfering bird food by stocking the seed in a tubular feeder hung from a tree branch on a wire that is about 10 feet long. The feeder should be positioned so that it is distant from any limbs or structures from which the animals might leap. If a squirrel learns to slide down the support wire, a plastic or metal dome can be placed atop the feeder. If the feeder must be placed atop a pole, then a dome baffle must be placed beneath the feeder.

A commercial bird feeder now on the market is constructed of metal and features a pressure-sensitive perch. When triggered by the weight of a squirrel, the perch tilts, causing a door to close over the mouth of the feeder.

If squirrels overcome all attempts to stop their raids on feeders, then the homeowner should not stock the feeders during the spring or summer. By the time fall arrives the squirrels may have "forgotten" how to maneuver around the baffle.

Squirrel Damaging Outdoor Plants—Squirrels rarely do really significant damage to plantings, so make certain the damage is not being caused by another animal. Squirrels are only active during the day, so it should be possible to observe the damage happening. If the damage is occurring at night, it is not a squirrel doing the damage. Once a squirrel has been implicated, consider the possibility of preventing access to the affected plant. For instance, a fruit tree or small orchard that is isolated from surrounding trees may be protected by wrapping a 2 foot band of sheet metal around the trunk about 6 feet off the ground. Branches occuring below 6 feet may have to be trimmed also.

Commercial repellents are available that can be applied to plants and may be effective against squirrels (see Sources of Products Appendix). Follow the label instructions carefully.

VOLES

There are almost twenty species of voles, or meadow mice, in North America. Voles are mouse-sized animals with short, coarse hair varying in shades from brown to gray; the ears and eyes are small; and the tail is longer than the hind foot but shorter than the head and body.

NATURAL HISTORY

Habitat—Voles are generally found in open grassy areas such as meadows and hayfields. Generally, they are agricultural pests, but they occasionally become nuisances in residential and urban areas.

Diet—Voles forage year-round and do not hibernate. Their diet consists primarily of plant cuttings and succulent grasses, but seeds and fruits are also eaten. In winter, voles will gnaw bark from trees and sometimes cause them considerable damage.

Breeding—Breeding occurs throughout the year, and ten or more litters may be produced, with an average litter size of five. Because of their breeding potential, voles can achieve high population numbers in short periods of time. Periodically, exceedingly high numbers are achieved in what are called population irruptions or "mouse years."

In most states, voles are classified as unprotected species. Animals may be killed, captured, or otherwise controlled without special authorization from the state game department. The manner of control, however, must be safe and humane and must conform with any other applicable laws.

Voles are not considered to be a significant source for any infectious disease that can be transmitted to humans.

Damage usually occurs to vegetables and crops, with the large-scale grower more likely to suffer than the small. Fruit trees may be severely damaged by voles eating bark in the winter. Voles are located by signs of their activity. They make prominent runways through the grass and leave clippings and droppings along these paths at intervals. Runways often end at burrows, which are about 2 inches wide and always kept open.

Habitat Modification—Cultivation and cleaning of grassy areas adjacent to gardens and crops are useful prevention measures. Hardware cloth (¼ inch or less) or tree wrap can be placed around individual trees and buried 6–8 inches (see fig. 4). Small vegetable or ornamental gardens can be protected by a wire screen ground cover (see fig. 10).

Repellents—Voles can cause serious damage to ornamental flower beds by destroying the bulbs of plants such as lilies and tulips. Soaking bulbs before planting in one of the many commercially available bittering agents containing thiram can be effective in limiting damage to new plantings.

WATERFOWL

The term waterfowl refers to swans, geese, and ducks. Although many species of waterfowl can cause problems for farmers and lakefront-property owners, the animals most often at fault are the well-known Canada goose, the mallard, and a domestic species called the muscovy duck. The Canada goose is a large, plump bird with a brown body, black neck and head, and a large white cheek patch. The mallard, one of the most common ducks in the United States, is identified by a blue band, bordered by white, on its wings. The bright green head of the male (drake) is distinctive. The drab brown female (hen) is identifiable by association with the male. The mallard closely resembles two other species of ducks. An inexperienced observer should consult a popular bird guide to correctly identify waterfowl.

NATURAL HISTORY

Habitat—Most ducks and geese are migratory, although local populations may become resident and remain year-round at a location. All waterfowl require bodies of water, such as rivers and lakes, at some time of the year.

Diet—The diets of waterfowl are varied, but the birds whose activities conflict with the interests of humans are those that feed chiefly on grass, grains, and other vegetation. The dietary preferences of these animals are general enough to cause occasional conflict with homeowners, golf-course managers, farmers, and vegetable gardeners.

Breeding—Reproduction occurs in the spring, although signs of mating activity may begin much earlier. Hybridization between domestic ducks and mallards occurs, with the white domestic coloration combining with that of the wild duck. When excess drakes are found, competition for females may be especially severe and lead to harassment. Geese are strongly monogamous.

LEGAL STATUS

All waterfowl are protected under the federal Migratory Bird Treaty Act and its amendments. Permits are required to capture or kill nuisance waterfowl and must be obtained through state offices of the U.S. Fish and Wildlife Service. No state or federal permits are required to scare or repel nuisance waterfowl, but local restrictions may apply.

PUBLIC HEALTH

When they occur in large numbers, geese and ducks often contaminate areas with droppings, which can be a problem if left to accumulate. Botulism outbreaks in waterfowl involve a strain that rarely is injurious to humans.

TYPES OF DAMAGE

Damage can occur in all areas from feeding, trampling, and defecating. Nuisance problems are becoming more common in suburban communities, near lakes and reservoirs, and around golf courses.

CONTROL METHODS

Habitat Modification—Control of waterfowl requires, first, awareness and sensitivity to potential problems before they get out of hand. Supplemental feeding, while a pleasurable and sometimes helpful activity, often leads to overpopulation and dependency. Feeders should be aware of these possible negative effects, and strategies should be developed to prevent adverse situations from occurring. Where waterfowl problems already occur, exclusion and repelling practices can be applied.

Exclusion—Waterfowl can be excluded by plastic netting or light wire fencing, such as chicken wire, in areas small enough to be effectively treated. The birds may also depart from an area if trees or tall shrubs are planted along their line of flight between a pond and adjacent property.

Frightening—A variety of techniques can be used to scare waterfowl away from areas where they are causing damage, and the greatest effectiveness is usually achieved when a combination of these is used. Scarecrows and other foreign or novel objects work well and are most effective if designed to move or are relocated frequently. Like most animals, waterfowl quickly adapt to consistent stimuli. A number of automatic noise-making or exploding devices are on the market, which produce loud noises to startle birds.

One of the most effective frightening techniques for waterfowl is a plastic flag system. A 2 × 3 foot black plastic flag featuring a V-shaped slot is stapled to a 4 foot wood lathe. Several of these are distributed in the field or other area where problems are occurring. When distributed at a density of one to five per acre, these flags are reported to successfully repel waterfowl. With all waterfowl nuisance situations, it is important to begin early before birds establish feeding and activity patterns.

Radio-controlled model boats have been used with some success to harass waterfowl away from ponds and lakes. Beach balls and balloons featuring a bulls-eye type pattern, known as eyespot balloons (see fig. 14), have been used to frighten geese away from shoreline property.

The woodchuck is also popularly known as a groundhog. It is a large, bulky rodent, weighing from 5–10 pounds and measuring 16–20 inches, with a short tail of 4–8 inches. Coat color ranges from light to dark brown.

WOODCHUCKS

NATURAL HISTORY

Habitat—Woodchucks prefer to live around agricultural areas and are associated with fields and farmlands. They may live in wooded areas near meadows, however, and in suburban and urban areas where old fields occur. They are often seen in the grassy strips of land paralleling highways.

Diet—Woodchucks are vegetarians and primarily eat native grasses and other plants. They will eat a variety of vegetables and fruits and can pose problems in gardens and crop fields.

Breeding—Woodchucks breed in March and April, and a litter of usually four to six young are born about a month after mating. The young mature rapidly and are usually on their own by midsummer.

LEGAL STATUS

Woodchucks may be classified as either an unprotected species or a game animal under a state's wildlife laws. In most states, there are no regulations pertaining to the killing or control of these animals. The manner of control, however, must be safe and humane and must conform with any other applicable laws.

PUBLIC HEALTH

Woodchucks are not considered to be a significant source for any infectious disease that can be transmitted to humans.

TYPES OF DAMAGE

Woodchucks will occasionally damage garden or field crops; look for the animals themselves or their burrows.

Woodchucks are true hibernators and will not typically be seen between early November and late February.

Habitat Modification—Woodchucks are timid and easily frightened. Novel stimuli, such as a beach ball, left to move across a lawn or open area with the wind, or scarecrows, may intimidate them from moving into an area. Removal of cover around burrows can create insecurity and, with other methods applied simultaneously, promote movement out of an area.

Exclusion—Where woodchucks have burrowed under houses or outbuildings, one-way doors can sometimes be used to effectively exclude them (see fig. 2). Removal of undergrowth and grass cover by mowing may be effective around buildings and residences. Woodchucks are good climbers, and fences are only likely to be effective if the area to be protected is small. The fence should be buried about 1 foot underground to prevent tunneling under it and be 3–4 feet high above ground, protected by a single strand of electrified wire placed immediately in front of it at a height of 4–5 inches.

Repellents—Although there are no repellents registered for use on woodchucks, it may be possible to encourage burrow abandonment by a tin can or other container, containing a strong odorous substance, placed in the entrance to the burrow as far back as can be reached. Gasoline has been used in the past in this kind of application, but other less volatile substances such as pine oil should be tried. This method should not be attempted in spring or early summer because of the danger of harming young in the burrow.

Trapping—Woodchucks can be live-trapped and relocated as a last resort when damage is severe. Traps can be set early in the morning and baited with apples or fresh vegetables. Covering traps during transport will calm the animals, and relocation to a suitable habitat 3–5 miles away should temporarily relieve nuisance problems.

There are about twenty species of woodpeckers in the United States, each with distinctive markings and habits. They range from sparrow-sized to crow-sized but do have certain characteristics in common. Woodpeckers all have sharp, chisel-like bills, along with stiff tail feathers and strong claws that they use to prop themselves upright when clinging to the bark of a tree trunk or large branch.

Habitat—Woodpeckers are found in most habitats where trees are common. Some species prefer deciduous trees while others prefer conifers. Most species do most of their pecking on dead or dying trees and so are more common where these "snags" are available.

Diet—Most woodpeckers feed primarily on insects that bore into dead and dying trees, such as carpenter ants, bark beetles, and wireworms, which they can dig out with their powerful beaks. Many also eat plant materials such as nuts and other seeds, and some will cache food in tree cavities they have built for later consumption. Woodpeckers are readily attracted to bird feeders that provide suet and/or sunflower seeds.

Breeding—Woodpeckers use their beaks to excavate cavities in trees for nesting sites. In the spring, they lay their eggs and raise their young in these cavities. Both parents usually help to

WOODPECKERS

NATURAL HISTORY

dig the nest cavity and care for the young. During the cavity-building stage, in preparation for nesting, woodpeckers often drill many smaller holes that are never completed or used. Cavities are also constructed in the fall and used as roosting sites.

LEGAL STATUS

All woodpeckers are protected by federal and state laws. They may only be captured or killed with special permits issued by the U.S. Fish and Wildlife Service.

PUBLIC HEALTH

Woodpeckers are not considered to be a significant source for any infectious disease that can be transmitted to humans.

TYPES OF DAMAGE

Nine species are known to peck on man-made structures. Woodpecker damage to man-made structures falls into three categories:

Drumming—Woodpeckers do not sing to advertise their territories or attract mates as other birds do. Instead, they have drumming stations within their territories, usually solid dead branches, which produce a loud resonating sound when pecked by the birds. The resident woodpeckers visit these sites regularly and loudly announce their presence to other woodpeckers. The problem occurs when a metal gutter or trim board on a house is chosen as a drumming site and the bird drums at dawn and annoys the homeowners. This is the probable situation when the pecking is concentrated in one area, is persistent, occurs in the spring, and does not result in a cavity.

Feeding—Woodpeckers find their wood-burrowing prey by hearing the rasping sounds they make. If a structure is infested by insects, woodpeckers will drill small holes or grooves to extract them. These feeding holes will lead to the insect tunnels, which can be seen upon close inspection.

Cavity Building—As mentioned above, woodpeckers excavate cavities for nesting, roosting, and in some species, for food storage. These holes will be round and deep and often occur at loose knots in the siding. The birds often start a hole and then abandon it and start another. In some cases, they may be confused when the hole penetrates the board and insulation is encountered. Sometimes the cavity is completed and nesting proceeds in the wall of the building.

Drumming—Anything that will muffle the sound of the pecking on the drumming site will discourage the woodpecker. Smaller boards may be covered with cloth or foam rubber padding until the habit is broken. This may not be practical for a long gutter or board, and a better strategy may be to hang strips of cloth or foil that flutter in the wind and frighten the bird.

Feeding—The root of this problem is the insect infestation, and the woodpeckers are doing the homeowner a favor by drawing attention to it. Appropriate pesticide treatment, perhaps applied by a professional exterminator, is called for. After the insects are controlled, the damage should be repaired.

Cavity Building—This may be the most difficult problem to control, but several techniques have been successful. One thing to keep in mind is that the bird building a nest or roosting cavity is passing through a seasonal behavior pattern, and if it can be discouraged from completing a cavity in a building for a few days or weeks, it will prob-

CONTROL METHODS

ably fulfill its need elsewhere and stop trying to use the building. (There is no guarantee that the bird will not return next year, however.) Therefore, a combination of prompt repair of the damage as it occurs and a program of scare tactics usually works. Shallow holes can be quickly repaired with caulking or wood filler, which is usually available in a variety of matching colors from building suppliers. Larger holes (assuming no birds are inside) may be filled with wooden plugs or wadded window screen and then caulked. While repairing holes, also caulk any loose knots that may be in the area.

A woodpecker may be scared away by simply opening a nearby window and shouting or banging whenever the pecking is heard. Hanging strips of foil or cloth from the eaves may also frighten the bird from the wall below. A water hose may also be sprayed near the bird to frighten it. The area may also be covered with a sheet of plastic or wire to discourage woodpeckers.

Repellents—Some success at repelling woodpeckers has been reported by treating wood siding with wood preservatives containing pentachlorophenol, but this has not been rigorously tested. Another chemical, called ST-138, has been patented for use as a wood treatment that repels woodpeckers harmlessly, but it has yet to be approved by the U.S. Environmental Protection Agency. Once it is approved, ST-138 will be marketed by the WPR Company, PO Box 31, El Campo, TX 77437; (409) 543-6271.

Trapping—In extreme cases, offending woodpeckers may be trapped and removed by licensed bird banders after appropriate federal and state permits have been obtained.

Zoonotic diseases are those diseases shared by animals and humans. Approximately 150 zoonotic diseases are known to exist. Wildlife serves as a reservoir for many diseases common to domestic animals and humans. Persons engaged in wildlife-damage control should be alert to the potential for disease transmission from animals. Neither animal handlers nor the general public have reason to be alarmed or frightened, but everyone should respect the potential for disease transmission and use sound preventive measures. Generally, disease is more easily prevented than treated.

This discussion reviews common zoonotic diseases, including those ailments that are often erroneously cited as being closely linked to wildlife. Many zoonotic diseases are so common in nature, so rare in humans, or so mild in their symptoms, that wild animals pose a minimal health risk to people. The diseases in this chapter are grouped according to their causative agent or mode of transmission.

Most of the bacteria that cause disease in wildlife also cause disease in man. There are several important routes of disease transmission. The contamination of neglected minor wounds, abrasions, and skin lesions where the skin is broken serve as common portals of entry for microorganisms. These infections are frequently caused by mixed groups of bacteria, but they usually involve staphylococci and streptococci. Another important mode of transmission is the contamination of mucous membranes, primarily the mouth, with feces or urine. Most of these infections can be prevented by establishing good personal hygiene habits, such as thor-

HEALTH CONCERNS IN WORKING WITH WILDLIFE

Bacterial Diseases

ough hand washing and protecting open lesions on the hands and arms. It should be noted that even bruised areas will be more susceptible to secondary bacterial infections than normal skin.

BRUCELLOSIS
(Undulant Fever)

INFECTIOUS AGENT   *Brucella spp.*

HOST   White-tailed deer, foxes, raccoons, and many other animals.

TRANSMISSION   Contact with tissues, blood, urine, vaginal discharges, or fetuses of infected animals.

Brucellosis is a highly contagious infection in many animals. It usually begins as a septicemia (blood infection) localizing in lymph nodes, spleen, reproductive organs, and joints where it can persist for long periods of time.

TREATMENT   Streptomycin, tetracycline, or sulfonamides.

PREVENTION   Use protective gear, especially rubber gloves, when handling infected animals.

BUBONIC PLAGUE

INFECTIOUS AGENT   *Yersinia pestis*

HOST   Fleas; often found on rats and ground squirrels.

TRANSMISSION   Flea bites.

Wild rodents and domestic animals serve as the hosts to the fleas. The disease is endemic (indigenous) in the southwestern United States. Human plague is characterized by a vesicular lesion at the site of the flea bite, with subsequent regional lymphadenopathy or lymph node enlargement. It generally progresses to generalized systemic disease.

Antibiotics. **TREATMENT**

Active immunization may be necessary in endemic areas. **PREVENTION**

LEPTOSPIROSIS

Leptospira spp. **INFECTIOUS AGENT**

Skunks, raccoons, opossums, Norway rats, mice, and many other animals including domestic species. **HOST**

Bacterial penetration of abraded or lacerated skin by infected urine or contaminated water. **TRANSMISSION**
   The disease is relatively rare in humans. A mild form is characterized by fever, chills, malaise, and myalgia (muscle pain). In the severe state, it may appear as a meningitis.

None with complete remission. **TREATMENT**

Good personal hygiene, particularly avoiding contact with urine of wild species. **PREVENTION**

PSITTACOCIS
(Ornithosis, Parrot Fever)

Chlamydia psittaci **INFECTIOUS AGENT**

Birds. **HOST**

Fecal-oral contamination and inhalation of dried discharges and droppings from birds. **TRANSMISSION**
   The infecting organism is present in nasal discharges, droppings, and tissues

of infected birds. The droppings are the most common route by which the disease is transmitted to humans. It is commonly found in feral pigeons that appear healthy. Clinical signs in people include fever, headache, upper respiratory infection, and pneumonitis.

TREATMENT Tetracyclines (doxycycline).

PREVENTION When entering into a potentially infected area, for example, a pigeon roost, wear a mask to prevent inhalation of dust from the droppings. Also, practice good personal hygiene.

SALMONELLOSIS

INFECTIOUS AGENT *Salmonella spp.*

HOST Birds and reptiles.

TRANSMISSION Fecal contamination of mucous membranes.

Salmonella gastroenteritis is probably the most common zoonotic disease of humans. It is estimated there are two million cases annually in the United States. The organism is commonly found in animals, especially birds and reptiles. While the bacteria can grow in the fecal matter of most animals, infections usually result from consuming foods and beverages contaminated with the bacteria. More than half of all cases are transmitted through raw meats, poultry, and pork. The disease usually produces a gastroenteritis (intestinal infection) accompanied by diarrhea. Systemic disease may result but is not common.

TREATMENT Antibiotics based on culture and sensitivity of the microorganism.

Good personal hygiene.

TETANUS

Clostridium tetanii

No animal host.

Contamination through breaks in the skin from penetrating or crushing wounds.

Tetanus is an acute disease caused by the toxins produced in the body by *Clostridium tetanii*. The disease is characterized by tonic spasms of the muscle groups of the jaw, neck, and back. Untreated, there is a 70 percent mortality rate.

Vaccination with a primary series of three doses of tetanus toxoid and booster every ten years is highly effective. Acute wound-associated tetanus can be prevented by appropriate wound management, including active or passive immunization.

TULAREMIA
(Rabbit Fever)

Francisella tularensis

Rodents and lagomorphs (rabbits).

Handling infected animals and contamination of cuts, and ticks.

At the site of entry an ulcer forms, followed by enlargement of the lymph nodes. Severe systemic disease can lead to headaches, myalgia, chills, and fever.

Streptomycin.

Use rubber gloves when handling animals, especially rabbits, as protection from ticks.

Viral Diseases

Viruses are known to infect a wide range of hosts, including humans and wild animals. The usual mode of transmission and dissemination is through the direct contact or aerosol contact with others of their own species. Wildlife populations, such as waterfowl, experience epizootics (epidemics in wildlife) caused by viruses. Duck plague, or duck viral enteritis, may cause large die-offs in a localized area. People also experience viruses; for example, the upper respiratory viruses where epidemics are not uncommon. There are only a few viruses that are common to humans and wildlife; however, since they have no specific cure, they can be very serious.

RABIES (Hydrophobia)
(Bite Wound Disease)

INFECTIOUS AGENT *Rhabdovirus*

TRANSMISSION Bite wounds, aerosol in bat caves.

Rabies is almost always a fatal disease of mammals, including humans. The disease progresses from fever and malaise, to paresis and paralysis of the muscles, to delirium and convulsions and eventual death due to respiratory muscle paralysis. Domestic animals once formed the largest reservoir for the disease, but, since the 1960s, wildlife species, especially skunks, bats, foxes, and raccoons, have taken over that distinction. In 1986, 5,551 cases of rabies were reported in the United States. Of these, 91 percent were from wildlife species. Rabbits and squirrels are rarely infected. In 1986, no cases of human rabies were reported in the United States or Canada. The usual annual toll over the past twenty years averages two cases per year.

1. Cleanse with soap and flush the wound immediately to mechanically remove the organism.
2. Thorough wound cleansing under medical supervision.
3. Antirabies serum and vaccination.
4. Tetanus vaccination or antitoxin.
5. No wound closure.

Since rabies is such a uniformly fatal disease, emphasis should be placed on disease prevention. People working with wildlife regularly should consider preexposure immunization. Mass vaccination of any group can be very cost-effective. The Merieux Institute, Inc., has developed a human diploid cell origin vaccine that is highly immunogenic and effective. This vaccine has improved the positive response of the vaccine and lessened the overall side effects known with the old vaccines. The vaccine is USDA approved for 1 ml intramuscular injections in a series of three doses on days 0, 7, and 21-28, then boostered every two years. It is also approved for 0.1 ml injections intradermally in the upper arm at the same time intervals as the intramuscular administration.

Helminth Diseases

Helminths are worms. All species of wildlife carry their own complement of helminth intestinal parasites. Our domestic animals also have specific kinds of roundworms. There are two forms of disease produced by these parasites. Cutaneous larval migrans is a penetration of the skin with the parasite undergoing a localized migration in or just under the skin, creating an inflammatory reaction that is self-limiting. Visceral larval migrans occurs when the eggs of a parasite are ingested and further penetrate the intestinal tract, where they undergo a migration through the animal's organs. The amount and severity of the disease depend on the organs affected.

CUTANEOUS AND VISCERAL LARVAL MIGRANS

INFECTIOUS AGENT *Baylisascaris procyonis* (Raccoon Roundworm)

TRANSMISSION Skin penetration, oral ingestion of eggs.

The roundworm of raccoons is reported to infect at least 70 percent of raccoons in some areas. For the raccoon, it causes few problems. However, it can cause serious illness to other animals, including humans. The adult worm can produce six million eggs per day, passing them in the host's feces. If accidentally ingested by another species, humans included, the larvae hatch and penetrate through the intestine, migrating to many parts of the body. If these larvae migrate into the eye, brain, or spinal cord, there can be serious, irreversible consequences. Blindness, central nervous system disease, or even death can result. Two children have died due to this migrating parasite. In adults, eye problems are a more common result.

Other species have roundworms that can sometimes penetrate the skin, causing a localized self-limiting skin irritation (Cutaneous larval migrans) in man.

Once contracted, the parasite is not treatable. Ocular lesions caused by *Baylisascaris* have been successfully treated with laser surgery.

1. Avoid contact with feces, especially raccoon. Use disposable gloves when handling fecal matter.
2. Good personal hygiene in handling any wildlife species.
3. Deworm all raccoons with an effective antihelminthic drug such as Strongid-T suspension (Pfizer) every two weeks, if they must be repeatedly handled.
4. Thoroughly clean and disinfect any cages, carriers, or areas occupied by raccoons.
5. Keep children from handling raccoons or from exposure to raccoon feces; e.g., cover backyard sandboxes.

These are one-celled animal parasites that infect both wildlife and humans.

Protozoal Diseases

GIARDIASIS

Giardia lamblia

Fecal contamination of water and hand-to-mouth transfer of cysts from feces of an infected animal.

A protozoal infection of the small bowel is often asymptomatic but may be associated with a variety of intestinal symptoms: chronic diarrhea, abdominal cramps, bloating, weight loss, and frequent loose, pale stools. Both wild mammals and birds can harbor these organisms. They presumably have acquired the disease from infected waters. Waterfowl and aquatic species of mammals are most frequently infected.

TREATMENT	Metronidazole.
PREVENTION	1. Avoid any hand-to-mouth contact while handling any wildlife species. 2. Good personal hygiene and hand washing.

HISTOPLASMOSIS

INFECTIOUS AGENT	*Histoplasma capsulatum*
TRANSMISSION	Inhalation of infective spores.

Histoplasm capsulatum is widely distributed throughout the United States. The Mississippi and Ohio River valleys are areas of high concentration. The organism thrives in the soil that has been enriched by the presence of decaying bird or bat droppings. It is most likely to be found in roost areas that had been established for a minimum of three to five years. The organism grows in the upper 1–2 inches of the soil. When combined with moisture, roost areas are exceptional for the growth of *Histoplasma*. The disease is acquired through inhalation of airborne spores. Upon first-time contact, the person will become infected. The majority of people who become infected develop only mild respiratory infections and, once recovered, become somewhat resistant. More severe infections are encountered in heavily-contaminated environments. The acute disseminated form, most frequent in children, may result in death. Similar forms of the diseases occur in skunks, rats, opossums, foxes, and other animals.

TREATMENT	Amphotericin-B.
PREVENTION	Avoid accumulations of soil mixed with droppings from bats or birds. If occupation of such areas is necessary, use

masks or a self-containing breathing apparatus. Always wear boots and properly bag clothing for washing. As a last resort, contaminated soil can be treated with a 3 percent solution of formalin to kill the spores, but such treatment will kill other organisms in the environment.

TOXOPLASMOSIS

Toxoplasma gondii

Ingestion of the oocyst (egg); eating undercooked infected meat; transplacental infection in primary infections of pregnant women.

Although wild animals are often cited as infectious agents for toxoplasmosis, the domestic house cat is the only species that passes infective eggs in its feces. All other warm-blooded species may become infected but are not excreters of the infective eggs. Other nondefinitive hosts only become infective when they are eaten by another animal. The disease is seldom severe and usually is self-limiting. Acute disease may result in high fever, lymph node enlargement, muscle pain, and even death. A pregnant woman is particularly susceptible and, when infected for the first time, often passes the parasite on to her fetus. Up to 3,000 babies are born every year in the United States with ocular lesions produced from *Toxoplasma gondii*.

Tetracyclines are effective in the active stages of disease.

Confining cats will prevent their contact with wild species. Make certain to practice good personal hygiene and sanitation. To avoid children interacting with infected cat feces, keep backyard sandboxes covered.

Tick-Borne Diseases

Several species of ticks are responsible for transmitting diseases from wildlife species to humans. As these ticks develop from juveniles to adults, they parasitize several different hosts. In ticks, the infective organism is transmitted both from the female to her offspring and between stages of the tick's life cycle.

LYME DISEASE

INFECTIOUS AGENT   *Borrelia burgdorferi*

TRANSMISSION   Bite of ixodid tick

Lyme disease is a newly recognized disease transmitted by ticks common to deer. It was first recognized in the United States in the New England states. Lyme disease has been reported in forty-three states, with a majority of the cases occurring in California, Connecticut, Massachusetts, Minnesota, New Jersey, New York, Rhode Island, and Wisconsin. *Borrelia burgdorferi* produces, in most cases, a characteristic skin lesion, erythema chronicum migrans (ECM). This lesion often expands in a few days to form an erythematous patch, or annular lesion. Systemic signs are accompanied by malaise and fatigue, fever, myalgia, arthralgia (muscle and joint pain), headache, stiff neck, and lymph node enlargement. Occasionally, an atypical encephalitis may develop. Disease occurs in summer.

TREATMENT   Penicillin or tetracycline.

PREVENTION   1. Avoid contact with tick vector.
2. Wear protective clothing and use tick

repellent while in tick-infested areas.

3. Check yourself, especially unprotected areas, for the presence of ticks every two to three hours.

4. Remove ticks as quickly as possible with tweezers or a protected hand.

5. Cleanse the wound carefully after tick removal.

ROCKY MOUNTAIN SPOTTED FEVER

Rickettsia rickettsi

INFECTIOUS AGENT

Tick bite and attachment.

TRANSMISSION

Rocky Mountain spotted fever is characterized by sudden onset with moderate to high fever that persists for two to three weeks. Headache, chills, and rashes that progress to hemorrhages are common. The fatality rate is about 20 percent in the absence of specific therapy. With prompt treatment, death is uncommon. The disease is generally restricted to the summer months in areas where the dog tick (*Dermacentor variabilis*) and wild animal hosts are abundant.

Antibiotics.

TREATMENT

1. Avoid tick-infested areas.
2. Same as for Lyme Disease.

PREVENTION

The last group of health-related problems involves physical trauma from a wild animal. Whenever a wild animal must be handled, the procedure must be accomplished as safely and quickly as possible. Proper techniques must be employed to minimize the risk of personal injury while, at the same time, avoiding injury to the animal. Traps, catch sticks, caging, and other appro-

Physical Trauma

priate equipment may be necessary when handling a wild animal. Most of these animals will be extremely stressed, resisting every restraint attempt.

In the unfortunate circumstance that a person is bitten or scratched, he or she should cleanse with soap and flush the wound immediately, providing for a mechanical removal of potentially infective organisms. This should be followed by cleansing under medical supervision. The question of rabies should be addressed, depending upon the species of animal and vaccination history. After a bite wound, one of five courses should be decided upon:

1. Begin post-exposure rabies prophylaxis immediately.

2. Sacrifice the animal and examine the brain for rabies.

3. Place the animal under observation.

4. Determine when there is no risk of rabies and no action is necessary.

5. Receive a tetnus vaccination or antitoxin.

The advice of a physician should be sought to help make the best possible decisions regarding the management of the injury.

SOURCES OF PRODUCTS FOR WILDLIFE-DAMAGE CONTROL

CHEMOSTERILANTS

Avitrol Corp.
7644 E. 46th St.
Tulsa, OK 74145
(918) 622-7763
Ornitrol

CAGE TRAPS

Hancock Trap Company
PO Box 268
Custer, SD 57730
(605) 673-4128
Hancock Beaver Trap

Ketch-All Company
2537 University Ave.
San Diego, CA 92104
(619) 297-1953
All Purpose Trap

Morrison Manufacturing Corp.
Highway 175, Box 52
Morrison, IA 50657
(319) 345-6406
(800) 648-CAGE
Safe-N-Sound

Mustang Manufacturing Company
PO Box 920947
Houston, TX 77292
(713) 682-0811
Mustang Live-Catch Traps

National Live Trap Corporation
PO Box 302
Tomahawk, WI 54487
(715) 453-2249
National Live Traps

Reed-Joseph International Co.
PO Box 894
Greenville, MS 38702
(800) 647-5554

Seabright Enterprises Ltd.
4026 Harlan St.
Emeryville, CA 94608
(415) 655-3126
Smart Mouse Trap

H.B. Sherman Traps, Inc.
PO Box 20267
Tallahassee, FL 32316
(904) 562-5566
*Sherman Small Mammal
  Live Traps*

Stendal Products, Inc.
986 East Laurel Rd.
Bellingham, WA 98226
(206) 398-2353
Arrestor #3

Tomahawk Live Trap
  Company
PO Box 323
Tomahawk, WI 54487
(715) 453-3550
Tomahawk Live Traps

M.S.I. Tru-Catch
PO Box 816
Belle Fourche, SD 57717
(800) 247-6132
Tru-Catch Traps

BALLOONS

Bird-X
730 W. Lake St.
Chicago, IL 60606-9864
(312) 648-2191

C. Frensch Ltd.
PO Box 67
Grimsby, Ontario L3M 4G1
Canada
(416) 945-3817

Raven Industries, Inc.
PO Box 1007
Sioux Falls, SD 57117
(605) 336-2750

Reed-Joseph International
Company
PO Box 894
Greenville, MS 38702
(800) 647-5554

EFFIGIES

W. Atlee Burpee & Co.
300 Park Ave.
Warminster, PA 18974
(215) 674-4900

Bird-X
730 W. Lake St.
Chicago, IL 60606-9864
(312) 648-2191

The Huge Co.
7625 Page Blvd.
St. Louis, MO 63133
(314) 725-2555

Smith & Hawken
25 Corte Madera
Mill Valley, CA 94941
(415) 383-2000
Scare Cat

ELECTRONIC ALARMS

C. Frensch Ltd.
PO Box 67
Grimsby, Ontario L3M 4G1
Canada
(416) 945-3817

Margo Supplies Ltd.
Site 20, Box 11, RR 6
Calgary, Alberta T2M 4L5
Canada
(403) 285-9731

Reed-Joseph International
Co.
PO Box 894
Greenville, MS 38702
(800) 647-5554

EXPLODERS, AUTOMATIC GAS

C. Frensch Ltd.
PO Box 67
Grimsby, Ontario L3M 4G1
Canada
(416) 945-3817

Harmon International, Inc.
Box 1827
Minot, ND 58702
(701) 839-6717

Margo Supplies Ltd.
Site 20, Box 11, RR 6
Calgary, Alberta T2M 4L5
Canada
(403) 285-9731

Reed-Joseph International
Co.
PO Box 894
Greenville, MS 38702
(800) 647-5554

H.C. Shaw Co.
PO Box 31510
Stockton, CA 95213
(209) 983-8484
Zon Mark II

KITES

McKinzie Scientific
PO Box 1077
Lancaster, OH 43130
(614) 875-7463

Sutton Ag Enterprises
538 Brunken Ave., # 7
Salinas, CA 93901
(408) 422-9693

LIGHTS, FLASHING OR REVOLVING

Bird-X
730 W. Lake St.
Chicago, IL 60606-9864
(312) 648-2191

R.E. Dietz Co.
225 Wilkinson St.
Syracuse, NY 13204
(315) 424-7400

The Huge Co.
7625 Page Blvd.
St. Louis, MO 63133
(314) 725-2555

PYROTECHNIC DEVICES

O.C. Ag Supply
1328 Allec St.
Anaheim, CA 92805
(714) 991-0960

C. Frensch Ltd.
PO Box 67
Grimsby, Ontario L3M 4G1
Canada
(416) 945-3817

Margo Supplies, Ltd.
Site 20, Box 11, RR 6
Calgary, Alberta T2M 4L5
Canada
(403) 285-9731

New Jersey Fireworks Co.
Rt. 7
PO Box 217
Elkton, MD 21922
(301) 398-2920

Stoneco, Inc.
PO Box 765
Trinidad, CO 81082
(303) 833-2376

Sutton Ag Enterprises
538 Brunken Ave., # 7
Salinas, CA 93901
(408) 422-9693

Western Fireworks Co.
2542 SE 13th Ave.
Canby, OR 97013
(503) 266-7770

RECORDED ALARM OR DISTRESS CALLS

Signal Broadcasting Co.
2314 Broadway St.
Denver, CO 80205
(303) 295-0479
(bird distress calls)

OTHER ACOUSTICAL REPELLENTS

Falcon Safety Products, Inc.
25 Cubbway Rd.
PO Box 1299
Somerville, NJ 08876-1299
(908) 707-4900
(air horns)

Tomko Enterprises, Inc.
180 Merritts Pond Rd.
River Head, NY 11901
(516) 727-3932
(*clapper* device with timer)

ELECTRIFIED FENCE SYSTEMS

Advanced Farms Systems
RD 1, Box 364
Bradford, ME 04410
(207) 327-1237
Techfence

Bay Mills Ltd.
Brampton Division
6 Holtby Ave.
Brampton, Ontario L6X 2M1
Canada
(416) 456-3394

Brookside Industries, Inc.
RR 1, Box 158
Tunbridge, VT 05077
(802) 889-3737

Gallagher Power Fence
PO Box 708900
San Antonio, TX 78270
(512) 494-5211
(800) 531-5908

Grassland Supply
Rt. 3, Box 6
Council Grove, KS 66846
(316) 767-5487

Jeffers Vet Supply
Box 100
Dolthan, AL 36302
(800) 633-7592
(800) 461-2836

Kencove Fence
111 Kendell St.
Blairsville, PA 15717
(800) 245-6902

Kiwi Fence Systems, Inc.
RD #2, Box 51A
Waynesburg, PA 15370
(412) 627-5640

Livewire Products
1127 East St.
Merrisville, CA 95901
(916) 743-9045

Margo Supplies Ltd.
Site 20, Box 11, RR 6
Calgary, Alberta T2M 4L5
Canada
(403) 285-9731

McKinzie Scientific
PO Box 1077
Lancaster, OH 43130
(614) 875-7463

Multi-Technical, Inc.
Tech Fence Division
PO Box A
Marlboro, NJ 07746
(201) 462-6101

Premier Fence Systems
Box 89
Washington, IA 52353
(319) 653-6631

Waterford Corporation
PO Box 1513
Fort Collins, CO 80522
(303) 482-0911
(800) 525-4952
*Shock Tactics Electric
    Fence System*

West Virginia Fence Corp.
U.S. Route 219
Lindside, WV 24951
(800) 356-5458

NETTING

A to Z Net Man
20 Universal Pl.
Carlstat, NJ 07072
(201) 488-3888

Bird-X
730 W. Lake St.
Chicago, IL 60606-9864
(312) 648-2191

J.A. Cissel Co., Inc.
PO Box 2025
Lakewood, NJ 08701
(908) 901-0300
(800) 631-2234

Conwed Corporation
Plastics Division
2640 Patton Rd.
Roseville, MN 55113
(612) 631-5700

C. Frensch Ltd.
PO Box 67
Grimsby, Ontario L3M 4G1
Canada
(416) 945-3817

Internet, Inc.
2730 Nevada Ave. N.
Minneapolis, MN 55427
(612) 541-9690
(800) 328-8456

Margo Supplies Ltd.
Site 20, Box 11, RR 6
Calgary, Alberta T2M 4L5
Canada
(403) 285-9731

ProSoCo, Inc.
PO Box 171677
Kansas City, KS 66117
(913) 281-2700

Quadel Industries
200 Tory St.
Coos Bay, OR 97420
(503) 267-2622

Wildlife Control Technology
2501 N. Sunnyside #103
Fresno, CA 93727
(209) 294-0262

PORCUPINE WIRE

Nixalite of America
1025 16th Ave.
PO Box 727
E. Moline, IL 61244
(309) 755-8771
(800) 624-1189

Shaw Steeple Jacks, Inc.
2710 Bedford St.
Johnstown, PA 15904
(814) 266-8008

OTHER EXCLUSION MATERIALS

3 E Group
PO Box 392
Moorestown, NJ 08057
(609) 866-7600
(bat excluding material)

Audubon Entities, Inc.
2179 E. Semora Blvd.
Suite 307
Apoka, FL 32703
(407) 889-0060
(*Bird Guardian* birdhouse guard)

Barrier Products
421-A Commercial Way
La Habra, CA 90631
(213) 691-9093
(*Bird Barrier* coiled wire)

Davlyn Manufacturing Co., Inc.
PO Box B
Springs City, PA 19475
(215) 948-5050
(*Tree Tender* tree wrap)

Hyde Bird Feeder Co.
56 Felton St.
Waltham, MA 02154
(617) 893-6780
(squirrel baffler)

Keystone Steel & Wire
7000 SW Adams St.
Peoria, IL 61641
(800) 447-6444
(fencing)

McKinzie Scientific
PO Box 1077
Lancaster, OH 43130
(614) 875-7463
(bat excluder)

Ol' Sam Peabody
PO Box 316
Berrien Springs, MI 49103
(616) 471-4031
(window silhouette decal)

REPELLENTS, TASTE

Burlington Bio-Medical & Scientific
Corp.
222 Sherwood Ave.
Farmingdale, NY 11735-1718
(516) 694-9000

REPELLENTS, ODOR

Animal Repellents, Inc.
PO Box 510
Orchard Hill, GA 30266
(404) 227-8222
(800) 241-5064

Bonide Chemical Co.
2 Wurz Ave.
Yorkville, NY 13495
(315) 736-8231

Dragon Chemical Co.
PO Box 7311
Roanoke, VA 24019
(703) 362-3657

Earl May Seed & Nursery Co.
208 N. Elm
Shenandoah, IA 51603
(712) 246-1020

Faesy & Besthoff, Inc.
143 River Rd.
Edgewater, NJ 07020
(201) 945-6200

Gustafson, Inc.
PO Box 220065
Dallas, TX 75222
(214) 931-8899
(800) 527-4781

Intagra, Inc.
8500 Pilsbury Ave. South
Bloomington, MN 55420
(612) 881-5535
Deer-Away

Miller Chemical and
Fertilizer
Box 333
Hanover, PA 17331
(717) 632-8921

Nott Manufacturing
PO Box 685
Pleasant Valley, NY
12569
(914) 635-3243

Planttabs Co.
Box 397
Timonium, MD 21093
(301) 252-4620
Scent-Off

P.K. Products
PO Box 1888
Paterson, NJ 07509
(201) 742-6468

Leffingwell Division
UNIROYAL Chemical Co.
111 S. Berry St.
PO Box 1880
Brea, CA 92621
(714) 529-3973

Wilbur-Ellis Co.
PO Box 1286
Fresno, CA 93715
(209) 442-1220

This section lists the
manufacturers and
distributors of products
discussed in the pocket
guide. No endorsement
of specific brands is
implied or intended. The
addresses and telephone
numbers are subject to
change without notice.
This list was developed,
in part, from information
provided by the Nebraska
Cooperative Extension
Service.

INDEX

Getting to Know The HSUS

Animals depend on us to protect them in a world that seems to have less and less regard for them. Whenever we encroach on animals' territory, or when we use our fellow creatures as commodities, the animal suffers. The Humane Society of the United States, a nonprofit organization, is devoted to making the world safe for animals through legal, educational, legislative, and investigative means. The HSUS is dedicated to speaking for animals, who cannot speak for themselves. We believe that humans have a moral obligation to protect the other species with which they share the earth. Founded in 1954, The HSUS, with a constituency of more than a million persons, maintains several regional offices, an educational division, a team of investigators, legislative experts, and an animal-control academy.

You Can Help...

You have the power to help animals. You can help animals with the choices you make every day. Think before you buy. Become a compassionate consumer by letting your purchases advertise your concern for animals. Shop for clothing and jewelry that aren't the products of cruelty. Don't buy fur, a frivolous fashion that causes unimaginable suffering to millions of animals. Do not use or buy ivory, the price of which is disappearance of elephants from the earth. Use cosmetics and personal-care products that aren't tested on animals. A wide variety of beautiful cosmetics is available that does not result from cruel laboratory tests on animals. Eat with conscience, thereby helping to minimize the suffering of animals used for food. Choose only tuna that is identified with a "Dolphin Safe" label.

Join The Humane Society of the United States as we work to give animals their rightful place in this world. Because, it's not just our world. The world belongs to the animals, too.

HSUS Programs

Wildlife—We file lawsuits and conduct other action programs to save wildlife and its habitat and to protect wildlife from inhumane and cruel treatment. Also, we publish books and conduct seminars to encourage the enjoyment of wildlife and to teach people how to live compatibly with wild animals.

Companion Animals—The HSUS promotes responsible pet ownership—including spaying or neutering of pets. Our nationwide campaign "Until There Are None—Adopt One" encourages the public to adopt their pets exclusively from animal shelters.

Laboratory Animals—The HSUS seeks to protect from suffering and abuse those animals now being used in research and to end all unnecessary and painful experimentation.

Farm Animals—The HSUS is working with the farm community, as well as with state and federal legislators, to end cruel farming and livestock rearing practices and promote humane sustainable agriculture.

Education—From its quarterly magazine, *HSUS News*, to its issue-oriented *Close-Up Reports*, The HSUS provides tools to help animals. The HSUS touches children, too, through its educational division, the National Association for Humane and Environmental Education (NAHEE), which urges students to be kind to animals and assists teachers with humane lesson plans.

Membership dues in The HSUS are only $10 per year. To join The Humane Society of the United States or for more information, please write The Humane Society of the United States, 2100 L Street, NW, Washington, DC 20037.